First World War
and Army of Occupation
War Diary
France, Belgium and Germany

74 (YEOMANRY) DIVISION
229 Infantry Brigade
Headquarters
1 May 1918 - 23 June 1919

WO95/3152/1

The Naval & Military Press Ltd
www.nmarchive.com
Published in association with The National Archives

Published by

The Naval & Military Press Ltd

Unit 10 Ridgewood Industrial Park,

Uckfield, East Sussex,

TN22 5QE England

Tel: +44 (0) 1825 749494

www.naval-military-press.com

www.nmarchive.com

This diary has been reprinted in facsimile from the original. Any imperfections are inevitably reproduced and the quality may fall short of modern type and cartographic standards.

© **Crown Copyright**
Images reproduced by permission of The National Archives, London, England, 2015.

Contents

Document type	Place/Title	Date From	Date To
Heading	WO95/3152/1 Headquarters		
Heading	74th Division 229th Infy Bde Bde Headquarters 1918 May-May 1919		
Heading	H.Q. 229th Inf Bde (74th Division) May 1918		
War Diary	At Sea	01/05/1918	07/05/1918
War Diary	In Train	07/05/1918	31/05/1918
Operation(al) Order(s)	Brigade Operation Order No.55 by Brigadier General R.Hoare D.S.O. Commdg 229th Inf. Bde.	19/05/1918	19/05/1918
Miscellaneous	Addenda to Brigade Order No.55 Of 19-5-18.	19/05/1918	19/05/1918
Miscellaneous	Addenda No.2 To Brigade Operation Order No.55 Of 19-5-18	19/05/1918	19/05/1918
Operation(al) Order(s)	Brigade Order No.56	24/05/1918	24/05/1918
Miscellaneous	March Table		
Heading	Headquarters 229th Inf Bde (74th Division) June 1918		
War Diary	Liencourt Area	01/06/1918	29/06/1918
Operation(al) Order(s)		24/05/1918	24/05/1918
Miscellaneous	March Table		
Operation(al) Order(s)	Brigade Order No.57	25/06/1918	25/06/1918
Miscellaneous			
Operation(al) Order(s)	Addenda to Brigade Order No.57	25/06/1918	25/06/1918
Miscellaneous	March Table		
Operation(al) Order(s)	229th Infantry Brigade Order No.58	27/06/1918	27/06/1918
Heading	Headquarters 229th Inf. Bde (74th Division) July 1918		
War Diary		01/07/1918	31/07/1918
Operation(al) Order(s)	229th Brigade Order No.59		
Miscellaneous	Table		
Miscellaneous	Addendum To 229th Brigade Order No.59	02/07/1918	02/07/1918
Miscellaneous	Reference Addendum To 229th Brigade Order No.59 para.6 No.2 Busnes-Steenbecque Line N. of Lys Canal	04/07/1918	04/07/1918
Miscellaneous	Administrative Instructions Issued In Conjunction With 229th Brigade Order No.59 And Addendum	02/07/1918	02/07/1918
Miscellaneous	Ammendment to Brigade Order No.59	03/07/1918	03/07/1918
Operation(al) Order(s)	229th Brigade Order No. 60	09/07/1918	09/07/1918
Miscellaneous	O.C. 16th Devons	10/07/1918	10/07/1918
Miscellaneous	Reference 229th Brigade Order No.60	10/07/1918	10/07/1918
Miscellaneous	March Table		
Miscellaneous	Administrative Instructions Issued In Conjunction With Brigade Order No.60	10/07/1918	10/07/1918
Operation(al) Order(s)	229th Brigade Order No.61	11/07/1918	11/07/1918
Miscellaneous	Reference 229th Infantry Brigade Order No.61 Dated 11-7-18	12/07/1918	12/07/1918
Operation(al) Order(s)	229th Infantry Brigade Order No.62	22/07/1918	22/07/1918
Miscellaneous	Table Issued With 229th Infantry Brigade Order No.62		
Miscellaneous	Administrative Instructions Relative To 229th Infantry Brigade Order No.62	22/07/1918	22/07/1918
Operation(al) Order(s)	229th Brigade Order No.63	30/07/1918	30/07/1918
Heading	Headquarters 229th Inf. Bde. (74th Division) August 1918		
Miscellaneous	Headquarters 74th. Division	16/09/1918	16/09/1918
War Diary	Busnes	05/08/1918	06/08/1918

War Diary	Carvin	06/08/1918	14/08/1918
War Diary	Labiette Farm	14/08/1918	14/08/1918
War Diary	Ham En Artois	16/08/1918	25/08/1918
War Diary	Q 19a 6.7	27/08/1918	28/08/1918
War Diary	Ham En Artois	28/08/1918	29/08/1918
War Diary	Behencourt	29/08/1918	31/08/1918
War Diary	B 26b9.5	31/08/1918	31/08/1918
Operation(al) Order(s)	229th Brigade Order No.64	06/08/1918	06/08/1918
Operation(al) Order(s)	229th Brigade Order No.65	10/08/1918	10/08/1918
Operation(al) Order(s)	229th Infantry Brigade Order No.66	15/08/1918	15/08/1918
Miscellaneous	Addenda to 229th Infantry Brigade Order No.66	15/08/1918	15/08/1918
Operation(al) Order(s)	229th Infantry Brigade Order No.67	22/08/1918	22/08/1918
Map	Map		
Operation(al) Order(s)	229th Infantry Brigade Order No.68	23/08/1918	23/08/1918
Miscellaneous	March Table Issued With Brigade Order No.68		
Miscellaneous	Administrative Instructions Relative To Brigade Order No.68	23/08/1918	23/08/1918
Operation(al) Order(s)	229th Infantry Brigade Order No.69	26/08/1918	26/08/1918
Miscellaneous	Table		
Miscellaneous	Administrative Instructions Relative To 229th Brigade Order No.69	26/08/1918	26/08/1918
Miscellaneous	229th Infantry Brigade Group Entraining Orders	28/08/1918	28/08/1918
Miscellaneous	229th Infantry Brigade Group Entraining Station Berguette		
Heading	Headquarters 229th Inf. Bde (74th Division) September 1918		
War Diary	C.25.b.5.2	01/09/1918	05/09/1918
War Diary	B.26.b.9.5	05/09/1918	06/09/1918
War Diary	Aizecourt Le Haut	06/09/1918	06/09/1918
War Diary	Templeux La Fosse	07/09/1918	07/09/1918
War Diary	Longavesnes	08/09/1918	10/09/1918
War Diary	Templeux La Fosse	10/09/1918	18/09/1918
War Diary	K.5.d.1.1.	18/09/1918	21/09/1918
War Diary	Templeux Quarries	21/09/1918	25/09/1918
War Diary	Bde. Hd. Qrs. Corbie	25/09/1918	29/09/1918
War Diary	Bde. Hd. Qrs. Bourecq	29/09/1918	29/09/1918
Miscellaneous	Narrative of Operations Carried Out By 229th Infantry Brigade From 1st To 16th September 1918	16/09/1918	16/09/1918
Miscellaneous	Narrative of Operations Carried Out By 229th Infantry Brigade From 17th To 25th Sept 1918	25/09/1918	25/09/1918
Miscellaneous	229th Infantry Brigade Casualties incurred during Operations September 2nd to September 25th.	25/09/1918	25/09/1918
Operation(al) Order(s)	229 Brigade Order No.70	02/09/1918	02/09/1918
Miscellaneous	Bde Order No.70		
Miscellaneous	229th. Brigade Order No.70	03/09/1918	03/09/1918
Miscellaneous	229 Inf Bde Order No.71	04/09/1918	04/09/1918
Operation(al) Order(s)	229th Brigade Order No.72	08/09/1918	08/09/1918
Operation(al) Order(s)	229th Brigade Order No.73	09/09/1918	09/09/1918
Operation(al) Order(s)	229th Brigade Order No.74	10/09/1918	10/09/1918
Operation(al) Order(s)	Brigade Order No. 75	16/09/1918	16/09/1918
Operation(al) Order(s)	229th Brigade Order No.76	17/09/1918	17/09/1918
Miscellaneous	Administrative Instructions Issued With Brigade Order No.76	17/09/1918	17/09/1918
Operation(al) Order(s)	229th Brigade Order No.77	22/09/1918	22/09/1918
Miscellaneous	O.C. 16th Division	20/09/1918	20/09/1918
Miscellaneous	229th Brigade Order No.77	22/09/1918	22/09/1918

Operation(al) Order(s)	229th Brigade Order No.78	24/09/1918	24/09/1918
Miscellaneous	March Table Issued With 229th Brigade Order No.78		
Miscellaneous	Administrative Instructions Reference This Office No.38 Of 26th Instant	26/09/1918	26/09/1918
Miscellaneous	Medical Arrangements No.12 74th (Yeomanry) Division.	26/09/1918	26/09/1918
Miscellaneous	229th Brigade Warning Order	26/09/1918	26/09/1918
Miscellaneous	Warning Order	27/09/1918	27/09/1918
Miscellaneous	Warning Order	28/09/1918	28/09/1918
Operation(al) Order(s)	229th Brigade Order No.79	29/09/1918	29/09/1918
Miscellaneous	Administrative Instructions Relative To 229th Brigade Order No.79	30/09/1918	30/09/1918
Miscellaneous	229th Brigade Warning Order	20/09/1918	20/09/1918
Heading	Headquarters 229th Inf. Bde. (74th Division) October 1918		
Miscellaneous	Headquarters 74th (Yeo) Division	03/11/1918	03/11/1918
War Diary	Le Cornet	02/10/1918	02/10/1918
War Diary	Pontlogy M.34c	03/10/1918	03/10/1918
War Diary	T4a1.7	04/10/1918	11/10/1918
War Diary	N 30 d 55	14/10/1918	15/10/1918
War Diary	O.28.a	16/10/1918	17/10/1918
War Diary	Q.26a	18/10/1918	18/10/1918
War Diary	Lezennes	19/10/1918	19/10/1918
War Diary	Pont A. Tressin	20/10/1918	20/10/1918
War Diary	O.20d24	21/10/1918	24/10/1918
War Diary	Luchin (M 36a)	25/10/1918	31/10/1918
Miscellaneous	Reference Brigade Order No.79	01/10/1918	01/10/1918
Miscellaneous	Bas Rieux-Busnettes-Gonnehem-Hinges thence to destinations		
Miscellaneous	A Form Messages And Signals		
Operation(al) Order(s)	229th Brigade Order No.80	07/10/1918	07/10/1918
Miscellaneous	March Table Issued With Brigade Order No.80		
Miscellaneous	Administrative Instructions Relative To 229th Brigade Order No.80	08/10/1918	08/10/1918
Miscellaneous	Administrative Instructions Relative To 74th Division Order No.97	08/10/1918	08/10/1918
Operation(al) Order(s)	229th Brigade Order No.81	08/10/1918	08/10/1918
Miscellaneous	Amendment To 229th Brigade Order No. 81 Dated 8th October 1918	10/10/1918	10/10/1918
Operation(al) Order(s)	229th Brigade Order No.82	10/10/1918	10/10/1918
Miscellaneous	Headquarters 229th Infantry Brigade	10/10/1918	10/10/1918
Miscellaneous	Small Local Operations	10/10/1918	10/10/1918
Operation(al) Order(s)	229th Brigade Order No.83	13/10/1918	13/10/1918
Operation(al) Order(s)	229th Brigade Order No.84	15/10/1918	15/10/1918
Miscellaneous	March Table		
Operation(al) Order(s)	229th Brigade Order No.85	23/10/1918	23/10/1918
Operation(al) Order(s)	229th Infantry Brigade Order No.86	25/10/1918	25/10/1918
Miscellaneous	March Table		
Operation(al) Order(s)	229 Infantry Brigade Order No.87	31/10/1918	31/10/1918
Miscellaneous	March Table To Accompany 229 Infantry Brigade Order No.87	31/10/1918	31/10/1918
Heading	Headquarters 229th Inf. Bde. (74th Division) November 1918		
Miscellaneous	Headquarters 74th (Yeo) Division	03/12/1918	03/12/1918
War Diary	Camphin	01/11/1918	08/11/1918
War Diary	Lamain	09/11/1918	09/11/1918

Type	Description	Start	End
War Diary	La Rosiere Farm. Q.9.C	10/11/1918	10/11/1918
War Diary	Cornet B.25.d	11/11/1918	30/11/1918
Miscellaneous	Addendum To 229 Infantry Brigade Order No.87	01/11/1918	01/11/1918
Operation(al) Order(s)	229 Infantry Brigade Order No.88	07/11/1918	07/11/1918
Miscellaneous	March Table To Accompany 229th Infantry Brigade Order No.88	07/11/1918	07/11/1918
Miscellaneous	Summary Of Information Concerning Section To Be Relieved		
Operation(al) Order(s)	229 Infantry Brigade Order No.89	09/11/1918	09/11/1918
Miscellaneous	March Table Issued With Brigade Order No.89	09/11/1918	09/11/1918
Operation(al) Order(s)	229 Infantry Brigade Order No.90	11/11/1918	11/11/1918
Miscellaneous	March Table To Accompany Brigade Order No. 90	11/11/1918	11/11/1918
Miscellaneous	Warning Order		
Operation(al) Order(s)	229 Infantry Brigade Order No.91	12/11/1918	12/11/1918
Miscellaneous	March Table To Accompany Brigade Order No.91	12/11/1918	12/11/1918
Miscellaneous	Addenda to 229th Inf. Bde. Order No.92	16/11/1918	16/11/1918
Operation(al) Order(s)	229th Brigade Order No.92	16/11/1918	16/11/1918
Miscellaneous	March Table To Accompany 229th Bde. Order No.92	16/11/1918	16/11/1918
Heading	Headquarters 229th Inf. Bde. (74th Inf. Bde (74th Division) December 1918		
War Diary	Leuze	01/12/1918	16/12/1918
Miscellaneous	229th. Bde	02/12/1918	02/12/1918
Map	Map		
Miscellaneous	Instructions For Advanced Billeting Parties	07/12/1918	07/12/1918
Miscellaneous	Warning Order	06/12/1918	06/12/1918
Miscellaneous	Administrative Instructions Reference Move Of 229th Infantry Bde. To Grammont Area	07/12/1918	07/12/1918
Miscellaneous	O.C. 16th Devons	10/12/1918	10/12/1918
Miscellaneous	To Headquarters 229th Brigade	08/12/1918	08/12/1918
Miscellaneous	O.C., 15th Devon Regt	10/12/1918	10/12/1918
Operation(al) Order(s)	74th Division Order No.118	10/12/1918	10/12/1918
Miscellaneous	March Table (To Accompany 74th (Yeo) Division Order No.118)		
Miscellaneous	Reference Divisional Order No.118	13/12/1918	13/12/1918
Miscellaneous	Headquarters 229th Inf. Bde. C.R.A.	13/12/1918	13/12/1918
Miscellaneous	Administrative Instructions Relative To 74th Division Order No.118	12/12/1918	12/12/1918
Miscellaneous	Administrative Instructions Issued In Connection With Bde Order No		
Miscellaneous	Administrative Instructions Relative To 74th Divisional Order No.116	13/12/1918	13/12/1918
Operation(al) Order(s)	229th Brigade Order No.94	13/12/1918	13/12/1918
Miscellaneous	March Table Issued With 229th Brigade Order No.94		
Miscellaneous	Administrative Instructions Issued In Connection With Brigade Order No. 94	15/12/1918	15/12/1918
Miscellaneous	Education Group No. 3 (229th Inf. Bde)		
War Diary	Grammont	07/01/1919	28/01/1919
War Diary	Grammont V.2.A.5.5	01/01/1919	31/01/1919
War Diary	Grammont	00/02/1919	00/02/1919
War Diary	Grammont V.2.a.5.5	01/02/1919	26/02/1919
Miscellaneous	Headquarters 74th (Yeo) Division	04/04/1919	04/04/1919
War Diary	Grammont	01/03/1919	31/03/1919
Miscellaneous	Headquarters 74th (Yeo) Division	05/05/1919	05/05/1919
War Diary	Grammont Belgium	00/04/1919	29/05/1919
Miscellaneous	Hqrs 74th (Yeo) Div	25/06/1919	25/06/1919
War Diary	Grammont (Belgium)	04/06/1919	23/06/1919

WO95/3152/1
Headquarters

74TH DIVISION
229TH INFY BDE

BDE HEADQUARTERS
1918 MAY - ~~DEC 1918~~
~~JAN~~ - MAY 1919

Vol. 2.

H.62.
229th Inf. Bde.
(74th Division)

May 1918

Army Form C. 2118.

WAR DIARY
or
INTELLIGENCE SUMMARY.
(Erase heading not required.)

Headquarters
229th Infantry Brigade

May 1/18

Place	Date 1918 May.	Hour	Summary of Events and Information	Remarks and references to Appendices
AT SEA	1st to 7th		Grant The Brigade less 229th L.T.M.By left ALEXANDRIA on board H.M.T. INDARRA	
In Train	10th		arrived MARSEILLES & entrained for NOYELLES	
			arrived at NOYELLES & were billetted as follows:— Bde HQ & No 2 Sec Div Sigs ST FIRMIN 229th L.T.M.B5 HAMELET 1/6th Devons FAYIERES R.A.R.E 12th S.L.I. FOREST MONTIERS BERNAY 12th R.S.Fus RUE 448 Coy Div Train —"— 14th R.H. ST FIRMIN RUE 229 FA	
	11th to 19th		Refitting & training	
	20th to 22		The Bde. moved to Sus-St-LEGER area and Relieves a by train (See Brigade Order No 55,) moved to Sus-St-LEGER area and Relieved coy details.(Ref LF.N.S.11) 16 Devons Sus St LEGER 14 R.H. HUMBER COURT 12 S.L.I. " 229 T.M.B. " 11 229 (B.G) " 12 R.S.F. COUHEMONT 448 Coy Div Train " 229 Fd. Amb. "	
	23 & 24		Trains continued.	

Army Form C. 2118.

WAR DIARY
or
INTELLIGENCE SUMMARY.
(Erase heading not required.)

Headquarters
229th Infantry Brigade

Place	Date	Hour	Summary of Events and Information	Remarks and references to Appendices
HQ 229 I.B.	1918 MAY 9.5		229 Brigade Group moved to the HIENCOURT Area according to Brigade Order No 56 of 24.5.18 attached.	
	26 to 31.		Training continued in a funeral improved training area.	

Alan Tuck
Captain
Brigade Major.

SECRET

Copy No 15

BRIGADE OPERATION ORDER No.55.

Ref.Map
N.W.Europe Sheets 3 and 4.
Scale 1/250,000.

By Brigadier General R.HOARE,D.S.O.,Commdg.229th Inf.Bde.

1. The 229th Infantry Brigade Group will move by rail from RUE on May 20th and 21st to the 1st Army Area according to attached table.
2. The Brigade Group will be billeted in the SUS-St.LEGER - HUMBERCOURT - COULLEMONT Area (A.3. and 4.)
3. Rations for consumption on 22nd instant will be drawn at Refilling Point RUE tomorrow, 20th instant, for those proceeding on 21st May.
4. Train timings will be forwarded as soon as possible.
5. Arrangements for carrying blankets will be notified later.

O.J.M. Tuck.
Captain,
Brigade Major,
229th Infantry Brigade.

Headquarters,
 229th Infantry Brigade,
  19th May 1918.

Issued at ...6.45 p.m.

Copies to :-

No.		No.	
1	74th (Yeo) Division	2	B.G.C.,229th Inf.Bde.
3	O.C., 16th Devon Regt.	4	O.C., 12th Som.L.Inf.
5	O.C., 12th Rl.Scots Fus.	6	O.C., 14th Rl.High'ers
7	O.C., 229th L.T.M.Battery	8	O.C., 229th Fld.Amb.
9	O.C., R.A.R.E.	10	O.C., 448th Coy.ASC.
11	229th Bde.Signals	12	229th Bde.Supply Offr.
13	Intelligence Officer	14	Brigade Major
15	War Diary	16	File

TRAIN TABLE.

May 20th

No.1 Train H.Q.& 74th Divl.Train, H.Q.,R.E., 985 Employment Coy. and 448th Coy.Divl.Train.

No.2 Train 229th Brigade Headquarters, No.2 Section Divl.Signals, R.A.R.E.

No.3 Train 16th Devon Regt - 27 officers 623 other ranks x. and 229th L.T.M.Battery

No.4 Train 12th Som.L.Inf - 24 officers 647 other ranks x.

No.5 Train 12th R.S.Fus. - 26 officers 540 other ranks x.

No.6 Train 14th R.H. - 24 officers 631 other ranks x.

x 51 animals and all transport wagons (less 1 cooker) and 3 G.S.Wagons of Divl.Train with their teams will accompany each battalion.

May 21st

No.7 Train Remainder of 16th Devon Regt, 12th Som.L.Inf. and 12th R.S.Fus. also 1 cooker with team and 1 G.S.Wagon and teams of each unit.

No.8 Train Divisional Headquarters.

No.9 Train 229th Fld.Amb, remainder of 14th R.H. with 1 cooker and team and 1 G.S.Wagon and team, and 59th Veterinary Section.

ADDENDA to BRIGADE ORDER No.55 of 19-5-18.

1. O.C., 12th R.S.F. will detail 3 officers to superintend the entrainment at HUM of the Brigade Group. One of these officers will always be on duty till the entrainment is complete. The Senior Officer will report to Lieut A.M.MONTGOMERY, Ayrshire Yeo. at R.T.O's Office HUM 3 hours before the time of departure of the first train. These three officers will travel by train No.9.

2. O.C., 16th Devon Regt will detail 3 officers to travel by No.1 Train to superintend the detrainment of the Brigade Group at LIGNY St.FLOCHEL. The Senior Officer will report to Lieut R.P.WOODS, Suffolk Yeo. on arrival. One officer will always be on duty until the detrainment of the Group is completed.

3. Special loading parties should be told off by Units and will accompany vehicles to the station.

4. Rations for day following the day of entrainment will be taken by troops

5. All Water-carts and Supply and Baggage wagons will be entrained full. The G.S.Wagons accompanying the last party of each Battalion will be filled with baggage and supplies.

6. All Transport including Baggage and Supply Wagons with loading parties will be at the entraining station 3 hours and personnel 1 hour before the time of departure of train.

7. Breast ropes and head collars will be provided for all animals entraining.

8. Entraining states will be prepared by all units and handed to the R.T.O. at the entraining station.

9. All Divisional Train Wagons will be returned to affiliated Train Company as soon as possible after detrainment.

10. All horses will be watered immediately prior to entrainment.

11. Detonated Bombs are not to be carried.

12. No lights are allowed when travelling in trains.

13. One Motor Ambulance will be present at both entraining and detraining stations.

14. Motor Lorries will be provided by 1st Army for the carriage of Packs of Troops proceeding to SUS St.LEGER, HUMBERCOURT and COLLEMONT.

15. Two motor lorries will report to each Battn. and one lorry to L.T.M. Battery for conveyance of blankets to HUM.

J.M.Tuck.
Captain,
Brigade Major,
229th Infantry Brigade.

Headquarters,
229th Infantry Brigade,
19th May 1918.

ADDENDA No.2 to Brigade Operation Order No.55 of 19-5-18.
----

1. Train Timings are as follows :-

    20th May   21st May

    No.1   0934   No.5   0134
       2   1344   6   0534
       3   1744   7   0934
       4   2134   9   1744

2. Motor lorries will be allotted as under :-
    20th May
    1 lorry Brigade Headquarters,   9.15 a.m.
    1 lorry T.M.Battery   9.20 a.m.
    2 lorries 16th Devon Regt.   2.   p.m.
    2 lorries 12th S.L.I.   5   p.m.
    2 lorries 12th R.S.F.   9.30 p.m.
    21st May
    2 lorries 14th R.H.   1   a.m.

3. All Waterbottles will be filled before entraining and unexpended portion of days rations will be carried.

19-5-18.
                                        Captain,
                                     Brigade Major,
                                  229th Infantry Brigade.

Distribution as in Brigade Operation Order No.55

SECRET

Reference Map
LENS, Sheet 11.

BRIGADE ORDER No.56

Copy No............

1. The 229th Brigade Group will move in accordance with attached March Table tomorrow, 25th May.

2. The Machine Gun Battalion, now at TERNAS is transferred to 229th Brigade Group.

3. Distances on the march will be maintained as under :-
    Between Battalions   500 yards
       "   Companies   100   "
       "   Unit and its
            transport   100   "
   First Line Transport will move with its unit.

4. Halts of 10 minutes will be observed at 10 minutes to the clock hour from 9.50 a.m.

5. Baggage Wagons will be drawn by representatives of units tomorrow morning from No.448 Coy. Divisional Train as follows :-
    Brigade Hd.Qrs.   1 G.S.Wagon & 1   At 7.30 a.m.
                       Lim.G.S.Wagon
    16th Devon Regt.   2 G.S.Wagons   at 7.30 a.m.
    12th Som.L.Inf.   2   do   at 7.30 a.m.
    12th Rl.Scots Fus. 2   do   at 6.45 a.m.
    14th Rl.High'ers   2   do   at 6.45 a.m.
   These wagons will be returned to Divisional Train as soon as possible after arrival in the new area.
   Distribution of Motor Lorries to units will be notified later.

6. Completion of move will be reported by cyclist orderly immediately upon arrival at destination.

7. All billets will be left scrupulously clean and latrines left in a sanitary condition.

8. Brigade Headquarters will close at SUS St. LEGER at 8 a.m. All reports after that hour to Brigade Headquarters in the line of march.

9. ACKNOWLEDGE.

                                    A. Ma. Tuck
                                    Captain,
                                    Brigade Major,
                                    229th Infantry Brigade.

Headquarters,
229th Infantry Brigade,
24th May 1918.

Issued at ...6-45 p.m...

Copies to :-
    No.1 B.G.C., 229th Infy.Bde.   No.2 74th (Yeo) Division
       3 O.C., 16th Devon Regt.   4 O.C., 12th Som.L.Inf.
       5 O.C., 12th Rl.Scots Fus.   6 O.C., 14th Rl.High'ers
       7 O.C., 229th L.T.M.Battery   8 O.C., 229th Fld.Amb.
       9 O.C., 448th Coy.Divl.Train   10 O.C., 439 Coy.Cheshire R.E.
      11 O.C., 74th Div.M.G.Battn.   12 O.C., No.2 Sec.Divl.Sigs.
      13 229th Bde.Supply Officer   14 Brigade Major,
      15 Staff Captain   16 Bde.Orderly Officer
      17 War Diary   18 File.

MARCH TABLE.

Unit.	From.	To.	Starting Point.	Time to pass S.Pt.	Route.
12th Som.Light Inf.	SUS - St - LEGER	LIGNEREUIL	Road Junction ½ mile S. of T in BEAUDRICOURT on SUS-St-LEGER - GRAND RULLECOURT Road.	8.45 a.m.	GRAND RULLECOURT
16th Devon Regt.	do	LIENCCURT		9.02 a.m.	do
229th Bde.H.Q. and No. 2 Sect.Div.Sig.Coy.	do	LIGNEREUIL		9.16 a.m.	do
448th Coy. Divl.Train	do	LIENCOURT		9.18 a.m.	GRAND RULLECOURT
229th Field Ambulance	do	DENIER		9.25 a.m.	do
229th L.T.M.Battery	HUMBERCOURT	LIENCOURT	Unit Alarm Post.	9.00 a.m.	GRAND RULLECOURT
14th Royal Highlanders	do	GRAND RULLECOURT.	do		direct
12th Rl.Scots Fus.	COULLEMONT	do	do	9.04 a.m.	direct
439 Coy.Cheshire R.E.	BERLENCOURT	do	do	9.21 a.m.	LIENCOURT
74th Machine Gun Battn.	TERNAS	BEAUFORT	do	9.30 a.m.	MAIZIERES -1- GIVENCHY -1- NOBLE
				8.30 a.m.	

Vol. 3.

"Headquarters,
229th Inf. Bde.
(74th Division)

June 1918

WAR DIARY / INTELLIGENCE SUMMARY

Army Form C. 2118.

Headquarters
2/2 Inf. Bde.
Vol 3

Place	Date 1918	Hour	Summary of Events and Information	Remarks and references to Appendices
HIENCOURT AREA	JUNE 1 to 25		The 39th Inf. Bde. Remained in the HIENCOURT area from June 1st to June 25th and the training of the Brigade was prosecuted and continued. Full Days were carried out. Fetes were... During Field Days on June 1st and 15th 15 p.p.g. " " on June 7th and 22nd. A large number of vacancies for all sorts of courses were filled by the Brigade.	
			On June 21st The 1/2 R.S.F. left the Brigade and was posted to the 14th Brigade of the 31st Division at Fetcham Depot that they were no...	
			On June 23rd an arranged occasion to G.H.Q. 8th O.B. IMR/IMR/MSt letter & dressed a full stream from 966. OR to 700 OR; and 1st Section from the BnStrns.	
	26.		The Brigade moved by train to the WITTERNESSE - NTHZANN area to acknowledge with Brigade ack. no 57 of June 25th am... and arrived June 27.	

Army Form C. 2118.

WAR DIARY
or
INTELLIGENCE SUMMARY.
(Erase heading not required.)

HQ 229th Duf Coy

Instructions regarding War Diaries and Intelligence Summaries are contained in F. S. Regs., Part II. and the Staff Manual respectively. Title pages will be prepared in manuscript.

Place	Date	Hour	Summary of Events and Information	Remarks and references to Appendices
HQ 229 DB	June 1918 29th		12 S.M.E. and 16 Devons Bn. sent to advanced area in Tigris and J25a to be employed for work under C.E. XII Corps. June 27 28 and June 29th. A reconnaissance of the BUSIVE- -STEEN BECQUE area carried out by officers (same OR) from each unit of the Brigade.	
			O.I.M. Tuck Captain & Brigade Major.	

SECRET   Copy No...18...

BRIGADE ORDER No.56.

Reference Map
LENS, Sheet 11.

1. The 229th Brigade Group will move in accordance with attached March Table tomorrow, 25th May.

2. The Machine Gun Battalion, now at TERNAS is transferred to 229th Brigade Group.

3. Distances on the march will be maintained as under :-
   Between Battalions   500 yards
      "   Companies   100   "
      "   Unit and its transport   100   "
   First Line Transport will move with its unit.

4. Halts of 10 minutes will be observed at 10 minutes to the clock hour from 9.50 a.m.

5. Baggage Wagons will be drawn by representatives of units tomorrow morning from No.448 Coy. Divisional Train as follows :-
   Brigade Hd.Qrs.   1 G.S.Wagon and 1   at 7.30 a.m.
                         Lim.G.S.Wagon
   16th Devon Regt.   2 G.S.Wagons   at 7.30 a.m.
   12th Som.L.Inf.   2   do   at 7.30 a.m.
   12th Rl.Scots Fus 2   do   at 6.45 a.m.
   14th Rl.High'ers   2   do   at 6.45 a.m.
   These wagons will be returned to Divisional Train as soon as possible after arrival in the new area.
   Distribution of Motor Lorries to units will be notified later.

6. Completion of move will be reported by cyclist orderly immediately upon arrival at destination.

7. All billets will be left scrupulously clean and latrines left in a sanitary condition.

8. Brigade Headquarters will close at SUS St.LEGER at 8.a.m. All reports after that hour to Brigade Headquarters in the line of march.

9. ACKNOWLEDGE.

                                          A.M.Tuck
                                              Captain,
                                           Brigade Major,
Headquarters,   229th Infantry Brigade.
229th Infantry Brigade.
24th May, 1918.

Issued at ....

Copies to :-
No.1 B.G.C.,229th Infy.Bde.	No.2 74th (Yeo) Division
3 O.C., 16th Devon Regt.	4 O.C., 12th Som.L.Inf.
5 O.C., 12th Rl.Scots Fus.	6 O.C., 14th Rl.Highlanders
7 O.C., 229th L.T.M.Battery	8 O.C., 229th Fld.Amb.
9 O.C., 448th Coy.Divl.Train.	10 O.C., 439 Coy.Cheshire R.E
11 O.C., 74th Div.M.G.Battn.	12 O.C., No.2 Sec.Divl.Sigs.
13 229th Bde.Supply Officer	14 Brigade Major
15 Staff Captain	16 Bde.Orderly Officer
17 War Diary	18 File

MARCH TABLE.

Unit.	From	To	Starting Point.	Time to pass S.Pt.	Route.
12th Som.Light Inf.	SUS - St - LEGER	LIGNEREUIL	Junction Road Junction	8.45 a.m.	GRAND RULLECOURT
16th Devon Regt.	do	LIENCOURT	½ mile S.of T in BEAUDRICOURT on	9.02 a.m.	do
229th Bde.H.Q. and No. 2 Sect.Div.Sig.Coy.	do	LIGNEREUIL	SUS-St-LEGER - GRAND	9.16 a.m.	do
448th Coy. Divl. Train	do	LIENCOURT	RULLECOURT Road.	9.18 a.m.	GRAND RULLECOURT
229th Field Ambulance	do	DENIER		9.25 a.m.	~~LIENCOURT~~ do and LIENCOURT
229th L.T.M.Battery	HUMBERCOURT	GIENCOURT ~~RULLECOURT~~	Unit Alarm Post.	9.00 a.m.	GRAND RULLECOURT.
14th Royal Highlanders	do	GRAND RULLECOURT	do	9.04 a.m.	direct
12th Rl.Scots Fus.	COULLEMONT	do	do	9.21 a.m.	direct
439 Coy.Cheshire R.E.	BERLENCOURT	do	do	9.30 a.m.	LIENCOURT
74th Machine Gun Battn.	TERNAS	BEAUFORT	do	8.30 a.m.	MAIZIERES - GIVENCHY -le - NOBLE

SECRET W.D   Copy No. 17

BRIGADE ORDER No. 57

Reference Maps
Sheet LENS 11, Scale 1:100,000
 "   HAZEBROUCK, 5A, Scale 1:100,000
 "   51.c. Scale 1:40,000

1. (a) The 229th Brigade Group will move to the WITTERNESSE –
       HAZINGHEM Area by road and tactical train on 26th and 27th
       instant. There will be no "Omnibus Trains" available (see
       74th Division Letter C.A.237 of June 24th.
   (b) Units will be Billeted as follows :-
           Headquarters, 229th Bde.   LILETTE   (F.5)
           14th Royal Highlanders   FONTES   (E.5)
           12th Som.Light Inf.   RELY   (F.6)
           16th Devon Regt.   WITTERNESSE (W.5)
           229th Field Ambulance   LAMBRES   (E.5)
       x   448th Coy.A.S.C.   (probably   FONTES)   (E.5)
           439th Fld.Coy.R.E.   HAZINGHEM (E.5)
       x   229th L.T.M.Battery (probably FONTES) (E.5)

       x Location of these two Units will be notified on arrival
         at AIRE.

2. (a) Dismounted personnel of 229th Brigade Group will move by
       rail and detrain at AIRE. Full details as to entrainment,
       billets, and supplies will be notified later.
   (b) Mounted personnel will move according to Table overleaf.

3. The Machine Gun Battalion will join the 230th Brigade Group.

4. After arrival in New Area the 14th Royal Highlanders and 12th
   Som.Light Inf. will be placed under orders of the XI Corps
   for work. Details will be forwarded on arrival.

5. ACKNOWLEDGE.

                                              A Jn Tuck
                                              Captain,
                                              Brigade Major,
                                              229th Infantry Brigade.

Headquarters,
229th Infantry Brigade.
25th June 1918.

Issued at ... 1-30 pm

    Copies to :-
        No.1 B.G.C., 229th Inf.Bde.   No.2 74th (Yeo) Division
         " 3 O.C., 16th Devon Regt.   " 4 O.C., 12th Som.L.Inf.
         " 5 O.C., 14th Rl.Highlrs.   " 6 O.C., 229th L.T.M.Bty.
         " 7 O.C., 229th Fld.Amb.   " 8 O.C., 439th Fld.Coy.RE
         " 9 O.C., 448th Coy.A.S.C.   " 10 O.C., 229th Bde.Sigs.
         " 11 O.C., 447th Coy.A.S.C.   " 12 229th Bde.Supply Offr.
         " 13 229th Bde.Transport Offr.   " 14 Brigade Major
         " 15 Staff Captain   " 16 Intelligence Offr.
         " 17 War Diary   " 18 File.

Number.	Date.	Unit.	To.	Route.	Remarks.
1	June 26th	Mounted Personnel and Transport 229th Brigade Group. Order of March as shewn in para.1	TANGRY Station. Sub AREA	Via CUPLERS - MONCHY, BRETON - VALHUON. Starting Point Road Junction in C.10.b. Head of Column to reach Starting Point at 9.45 a.m.	Under Orders of Brigade Transport Officer who will report to Major HARDY, O.C. 447th Coy.A.S.C. at Starting Point. Billets from Sub Area Commandant - TANGRY (T.1) Units will take most direct route to Starting Point.
2	June 27th	As in No.1	WITTERNESSE - MAZINGHEM Area	No Instructions.	Under orders of Brigade Transport Officer.

SECRET   W.D.   Copy No...17...

ADDENDA TO BRIGADE ORDER No.57.

Ref.Maps
Sheet LENS 11, Scale 1:100,000
 "   HAZEBROUCK, 5A, Scale 1:100,000.
      51.c. Scale 1:40,000

With reference to Brigade Order No.57 :-

1. Units will march to LIGNY St FLOCHEL and TINQUE and entrain on June 26th 1918, in accordance with attached Table.

2. The following alteration will be made in the route shewn in March Table of Brigade Order No.57 of today's date :-

    Route :- Via AVERDOIGNT - BAILLEUL aux CORNAILLES - and MONCHY-BRETON.
    Head of Column to pass Church in BAILLEUL aux CORNAILLES at 10 a.m.
    All Mounted personnel and transport of 229th Brigade Group will be East of MAIZIERES - AVERDOIGNT - LIGNY-St FLOCHEL Road by 8 a.m.

3. Units will draw their G.S.Wagons containing rations for the 27th instant tonight.
    These waggons will be sent off in the morning with an advance party to be at the Entraining Station at 7.30 a.m. where these rations will be unloaded, and distributed to the men on the arrival of the Unit.
    The empty G.S.Wagons will then proceed to the Starting Point for the Transport (Church in BAILLEUL aux CORNAILLES).
    Refilling Point in the new Area will be at FONTES. Units will draw rations there at 6 p.m. on the 27th inst. and thereafter at 9 a.m.

4. The 448th Coy.A.S.C.,16th Devon Regt., 229th Fld.Amb. and 12th Som.L.Inf. will each detail a representative to be at Brigade Headquarters at 6.30 a.m. to draw one Motor Lorry for the conveyance of Blankets.
    These are allotted as follows :-

    (a) 16th Devons   ) 1 lorry
        229th L.T.M.Batty.   )

    (b) 448th Coy.A.S.C.   )
        14th R.E.   ) 1 lorry
        439th Fld.Coy.R.E.   )

    (c) Bde.Headquarters   ) 1 lorry
        229th Fld.Amb.   )

    (d) 12th Som.L.Inf.   1 lorry

    Loading parties of 2 men per Unit (one only from 448th Coy. A.S.C. and 439th Fld.Coy.R.E.) will travel on the lorries. When the Lorries are loaded they will Rendezvous at Brigade Headquarters at LIGNEREUIL.
    Sic Men going by Bus will take their blankets with them.
    Waterproof Sheets will be carried on the man.

5. Halts for 10 minutes at 10 minutes to the clock hour will be observed.

6. An Officer of each Unit will report to the R.T.O. at Entraining Station one half hour before the arrival of Unit and hand over Entraining State.

7. Completion of Move will be reported immediately upon arrival at destination.

/8.

8. Brigade Headquarters will close at LIGNEREUIL at 8 a.m. Reports after that time to Head of the Column.

9. ACKNOWLEDGE.

                                                  Tuck
                                                 Captain,
                                             Brigade Major,
Headquarters,   229th Infantry Brigade.
229th Infantry Brigade,
25th June 1918.

Issued at ....

Copies to :-
  No.1 B.G.C. 229th Inf.Bde.   No.2 74th (Yeo) Division
    3 O.C., 16th Devon Regt.   4 O.C., 12th Som.L.Inf.
    5 O.C., 14th Rl.Highlrs.   6 O.C., 229th L.T.M.Bty.
    7 O.C., 229th Field Amb.   8 O.C., 439th Fld.Coy.R.E.
    9 O.C., 448th Coy.A.S.C.   10 O.C., 229th Bde.Sigs.
   11 O.C., 447th Coy.A.S.C.   12 229th Bde.Supply Officer
   13 229th Bde.Transport Offr.   14 Brigade Major
   15 Staff Captain   16 Intelligence Offr.
   17 War Diary   18 File.

MARCH TABLE.

Train No.	Unit.	From.	To Entraining Station at.	Starting Point.	Time to pass Starting Point.	Route.
1	Hd.Qrs. 229th Bde. No.2 Sect.Div.Sig. Coy.	LIGNEREUIL	LIGNY St FLOCHEL	Cross Roads at G.25.a.8.6.	7.30 a.m. 7.30 a.m.	AVTRDOINGT. do
1 1 1	16th Devon Regt. 229th L.T.M.Bty. 448th Coy.A.S.C.	LIENCOURT	do	do	7.33 a.m. 7.45 a.m. 7.46 a.m.	do
1	14th Rl.Highlrs.	GRAND RULLECOURT	do	do	8.00 a.m.	do
2	12th Som.L.Inf.	LIGNEREUIL	TINQUES	Most direct route, so as to reach Entraining Station by 10.30 a.m. Precedence on the Line of March being given in order shown.		
2	229th Field Amb.	DENIER	do			
2	459th Fld.Coy.R.E.	GRAND RULLECOURT.				

NOTE :- Distances on the Line of March in accordance with Divisional Standing Orders will be maintained.

SECRET.   Copy No.....

Ref.Map Sheet 36 A Scale 1:40,000

229th INFANTRY BRIGADE ORDER No.58.

1. 74th Division will be held at 4 hours notice for the purpose of reinforcing either XI or XIII Corps.
   229th Infantry Brigade will be held at 3 hours notice - Daily, between 5.30 a.m. and 7.30 a.m. at 1½ hours notice.

2. The Division remains at 24 hours notice for the purpose of G.H.Q. Reserve.

3. Reconnaissances will be carried out as per para.6.

4. (a) In case of emergency, from midnight June 27/28th, the B.G.C.229th Infantry Brigade will command the Nucleus Garrison of the switch line along the Aire Canal, and the BUSNES - STEENBECQUE line in the XI Corps Area.
   Garrison will consist of 229th Inf.Bde. 'C' Coy.74th M.G.Battn. 1 Coy. 39th M.G.Battn.
   (b) On receipt of the order to move to Battle Stations, 229th Inf. Bde. will move at once as follows :-
   12th Som.L.Inf. to Canal Bank from Drawbridge in P.29.c.7.2. inclusive, to Drawbridge in P.20.Central inclusive, Route - St.HILAIRE - BOURECQ - immediately North of LILLERS - BUSNES, to Canal in P.27.b.central.
   16th Devons from Drawbridge P.20.Central exclusive to Railway P.8.Central inclusive Route - LAMBRES - MOLINGHEM - GUARBECQUE - HAMET BILLET.
   14th Rl.Highlrs. Railway in P.8.central exclusive to LYS Canal J.32.inclusive, Route - BERGUETTE, GUARBECQUE, St.VENANT Road in P.8.a. and P.2.b.
   14th R.H. will have precedence over 16th Devons by road.
   'C' Coy. 74th M.G.Battn. 2 Sections to HAMET BILLET (P.14.a.) 2 Sections to St.VENANT Road in P.8.a.
   229th L.T.M.Battery in vicinity of House in O.36.a.8.8.
   229th Brigade Headquarters. House in O.36.a.8.8.

5. Infantry where possible, will make use of cross country tracks along Canal Banks.

6. The following Officers will make a Reconnaissance of the Line today 27-6-18 :-
   Commanding Officers, Adjutants and Coy.Commanders of each Battn.
   Two Officers 'C' Coy. 74th M.G.Battn.
   C.O., 229th L.T.M.Battery
   One Orderly per Battn. and M.G.Coy.
   Steel Helmets, S.B.Rs. Haversack Rations and Sheet 36.A. Scale 1:40,000 will be brought.

7. A Lorry will leave Brigade Headquarters at 7.30 a.m. and pick up Officers in the following order :-
   16th Devons
   'C' Coy. M.G.Battn.
   12th S.L.Inf.
   14th R.Highlrs.
   229th L.T.M.Batty.
   The officer from 229th L.T.M.B. will parade with party from 14th R.H. The party will proceed under Lt.Col.G.S.POOLE,D.S.O. to Rendezvous at Drawbridge in P.20.Central where they will meet B.G.C. 229th Infantry Brigade.

8. "B" Teams will be earmarked forthwith.

9./

9. ACKNOWLEDGE.

                          (Sgd) A.J.M.Tuck, Capt.
                                Brigade Major,
Issued at 2 p.m.   229th Infantry Brigade.

Headquarters, 229th Inf.Bde.
   27-6-18.

Copies to :-
- No.1 B.G.C., 229th Inf.Bde.
- 2 O.C., 16th Devons
- 3 O.C., 12th Som L.Inf.
- 4 O.C., 14th R.Highlrs.
- 5 O.C., 229th L.T.M.Batty.
- 6 O.C., 74th M.G.Battn.
- 7 Office.

Vol. 4.

Headquarters,
229th Inf. Bde.
(74th Division)

July 1918.

War Diary of HAZEBROUCK 5a 1/40,000
36a 1/40,000

WAR DIARY
or
INTELLIGENCE SUMMARY

Army Form C. 2118.

July 1918
H.Q. 229ᵃ Inf Bde

Place	Date	Hour	Summary of Events and Information	Remarks and references to Appendices
	July 1ˢᵗ		Reconnaissances of the forward lines continued as for previous days in the area of the FORÊT de NIEPPE and the area south of HINGES and MERVILLE area.	
	7ᵗʰ			
	11ᵗʰ		2/4 R.H. relieves the 2/5ᵗʰ I.B. withdrawn into Divisional Reserve. Reconnaissances of the front were continued. 229ᵗʰ Bde Staff being unable to attend	
	22/23		2/4 R.H.I.B. relieved by 2/8ᵗʰ I.B. in the ROSIÈRE (Right) Sector of the line. Details of relief and disposition in the Bde war [?]	
	23/24		2/4ᵗʰ I.B. relieved by 2/8ᵗʰ I.B. in the ROSIÈRE (Right) Sector of the line. Details of relief and dispositions in the Bde war diary Brigade Orders no. 68 attached. Remaining Battalions	
	30/31		2/4ᵗʰ & 14ᵗʰ R.H. relieves the 1/5 Som.L.I. in the right subsector of the line. 16ᵗʰ Devons remain in line under left.	

H.Q. 229ᵗʰ Inf. Bde.

[signature]
Brigadier General
Comdg 229ᵗʰ Inf Bde

SECRET

Map Ref.Sheet 36A.
Scale 1:40,000.

229th BRIGADE ORDER No. 59

Copy No...... 18

1. Brigade Order No.58 and this office letter No.58a of June 28th are cancelled.

2. (a) 74th Division will be at four hours notice for the purpose of reinforcing either the XI or XIII Corps.
   (b) 229th Brigade Group will be held at three hours notice.

3. The 74th Division will be at twenty-four hours notice for the purpose of G.H.Q.Reserve.

4. In case of emergency, 229th Infantry Brigade and 'C' Coy.74th Battn.M.G.C. are placed at the disposal of G.O.C.XI Corps.

5. (a) On receipt of order to "MAN BATTLE STATIONS", the 229th Infantry Brigade will concentrate in one of three localities from which it can man, or supply nucleus garrisons for the BUSNES - STEENBECQUE Line.
   These localities will be as follows, and will be such that the Right, Centre, or Left of the Line can be manned as the tactical situation developes.
   Right,Area. LE CORNET BRASSART - LE CORNET BOURDOIS - LA MIQUELLERIE all inclusive.
   Centre,Area. TREZENNES - LA LACQUE - ISBERGUES all inclusive.
   Left,Area. BOESEGHEM - STEENBECQUE - THIENNES - all inclusive.
   (b) The telegram or message to "MAN BATTLE STATIONS" will be worded as follows to indicate in which area the Brigade is to concentrate, and will be repeated to 5th and 61st Divisions.
       e.g., "MAN BATTLE STATIONS" - CONCENTRATE RIGHT, CENTRE or LEFT, as the case may be.
   (c) Enclosed fields adjoining roads and with protection from Aeroplane observation are allotted to Units as follows in the Right, Centre, and Left Concentration Localities.
   These fields will be reconnoitred forthwith.

Unit.	Right Locality.	Centre Locality.	Left Locality.
	o	x	*
Bde.Hd.Qrs.	House O.36.a.8.8.	House I.31.d.8.7.	House I.16.c.2.2.
12th S.L.I.	O.36.b.3.7.	I.31.d.5.3.	I.16.a.8.2.
14th R.H.	O.30.c.3.3. & 3.5.	I.31.d.5.5.	I.16.a.8.6.
16th Devons	O.30.c.5.7.	I.31.d.8.8.	I.16.b.1.9.
'C' Coy.M.G.Bn.	O.36.a.7.7.	I.31.d.6.8.	I.16.a.8.4.
229th L.T.M.B.	O.36.a.8.9.	I.31.d.6.8.	I.16.a.7.4.
2 Sects.439th Fld.Coy.R.E. with 16th Devons	O.36.b.3.7.	E.31.d.6.8.	I.16.a.7.4.
229th Field Amb.	O.36.a.8.8.	I.31.d.8.8.	I.16.a.8.4.

o= So called Chateau. x House at Level Crossing. * Extaminet at Road Junction.

6. "Man Battle Positions, and Concentrate Right, Centre or Left" (as the case may be). On this Command being given troops will move to the Concentration Locality ordered, and form up in their previously allotted sites.
   The object of this is to keep the Brigade more closely under the Brigade Commanders control, until the actual direction of the attack is known, or instructions are received for the troops to move elsewhere.
   On it becomming evident that the attack is on our front, troops will move to the positions allotted to them.

/7.

7. **Action in case of Attack.** The chief duties of 229th Infantry Brigade are :-
   (a) To form a Nucleus Garrison in one of the systems of trenches and then to act as guides to any troops withdrawing from the front line, so that in no case may such troops pass through these prepared positions without halting to defend them, and similarly, to guide other troops coming up from the rear to reinforce the line.
   It is of the utmost importance therefore that all officers, N.C.O's, Scouts and Runners should become well acquainted with all roads, tracks, and bridges in the vicinity of their Sector.
   (b) If attacked, the line to stand fast and every foot of ground will be contested. Any penetration of our lines by the enemy will be immediately counter attacked, and for this purpose all Commanders down to Company Commanders will keep a Reserve in hand. The Plan of Attack must not be left till the last moment, but contingencies must be foreseen and thought out, and all routes of approach reconnoitred - "Always have a Plan".
   (c) the Brigade may be called upon to deliver a Counter Attack.

8. 439th Field Coy. R.E. (less two sections) will remain in its present location and await further orders.
   First Line Transport will in all cases move with its Unit.
   In the event of a Unit moving by bus or lorry, 1st Line Transport will follow by road immediately.

9. Lorries, if available, will be provided for the move of the 14th R.H., 229th Bde.Hd.Qrs. 229th L.T.M.bty. and 'C' Coy. 74th Bn. M.G.C., to the Left Concentration Area, but Units will be prepared to move by march route.

10. (a) The Reconnaissances which are being carried out will continue according to priority shewn in the attached table showing Sectors allotted to Units.
    (b) Tracings are attached of the first four of the systems in attached table.
    (c) Detailed orders for the reconnaissances to be carried out each day, will be issued the day before.

11. (a) Infantry wherever possible will avoid roads and make use of Cross Country Tracks and Routes along canal banks, and the shortest routes to the BUSNES - STEENBECQUE and AMUSOIRES - HAVERSKERQUE - LA MOTTE Line from the Concentration areas. These tracks and routes will be reconnoitred forthwith and marked by the Units concerned.
    (b) O.C.Units will forward to this office by 6 p.m. July 4th a Table showing :-
        i. Routes from Areas occupied at present to sites allotted in Concentration Areas.
        ii. Routes from sites allotted in Concentration Areas to each of the first four trench systems shewn in attached Table.

12. O.C.Units will prepare a Scheme and have orders issued for the action to be taken on receipt of the order to "Man Battle Stations" in any one of the Concentration Areas, and forward a copy of these orders to this Headquarters by 6 p.m. July 4th.

13. The 5th Division will warn the 12th Som.L.Inf. (less two Coys) and 16th Devon Regt, and the 61st Division will warn the two Coys Som.L.Inf. at St.VENANT and BUSNES of the receipt of the Order to "MAN BATTLE STATIONS". These Units will then march to the Concentration Area ordered, and take up their allotted position in accordance with para 5c.
    In like manner, 16th Devon Regt. will be responsible for warning the two Sections 439th Fld.Coy. R.E. of the Order to "MAN BATTLE STATIONS."

-2-

14. ACKNOWLEDGE.

[signature: C.J.M. Tuck]

Captain,
Brigade Major,
229th Infantry Brigade.

H.Q. 229th Inf Bde
July 13th 8-30 pm

Issued at..........

Copies to :-

    No. 1   B.G.C., 229th Infy.Bde.
        2   74th (Yeo) Div.
    x 3   16th Devon Regt.
    x 4   12th Som.L.Inf.
    x 5   14th Rl.Highlrs.
    x 6   229th L.T.M.Bty.
    x 7   'C' Coy. 74th Bn.M.G.C.
        8   74th Battn.M.G.C.
        9   229th Field Amb.
    x 10)
      11) 439th Fld.Coy.R.E.
      12   448th Coy.A.S.C.
      13   Staff Captain
      14   Brigade Major
      15   Intelligence Officer
      16   229th Bde.Signal Offr.
      17   War Diary
      18   File
      19   61st Division
      20   5th Division.

x Tracings sent only to Units marked with a cross.

TABLE

Reconnaissance number.	Line.	12th Som.L.Inf.	Sectors allotted to :— 14th Royal Highlrs.	16th Devon Regt.
1	BUSNES — STEENBECQUE South of LYS Canal	Drawbridge at P.29.c.7.2. to Drawbridge in P.20.central, both inclusive.	Draw bridge in P.20.central to GUARBECQUE — St.VENANT Road in P.2.d. both exclusive.	GUARBECQUE — St.VENANT Road to LYS Canal J.26.d. both inclusive
2	BUSNES — STEENBECQUE North of LYS Canal.	~~Drawbridge at P.20.a.5.5.xxx~~ LYS Canal in J.26.d. (inclusive) to ø J.14.c.20.	ø J.14.c.20. to Canal de la NIEPPE in J.7.d. (inclusive)	Canal de la NIEPPE in J.7.d. (exclusive) to Railway at D.25.d.4.5. (inclusive)
3	AMUSOIRES — HAVERSKERQUE — LA MOTTE. South of LA MALADRIE (J.34.)	Canal d' AIRE at P.35.b.9.9. to Junction of Trench and Road at P.17.d.4.6. both inclusive.	Junction of trench and road at P.17.d.4.6. to railway at P.11.a.9.8. both exclusive.	Railway at P.11.a.9.8. to ~~track~~ running E. and W. at J.34.b.4.2. *inclusive*
4	AMUSOIRES — HAVERSKERQUE — LA MOTTE. North of LA MALADRIE. (J.34.)	Brickfield in J.34.d. (inclusive) to S.side of BOIS MOYEN exclusive.	System through BOIS MOYEN.	N.side of BOIS MOYEN exclusive to Junction of trench with road in L.30.d.
5	LILLERS — STEENBECQUE.	A general knowledge by all Units from U.5.Central to C.30.central.		

ø Definite boundary mark has been decided upon by O's.C.14th R.H. and 12th S.L.I. and will be notified shortly. *the boundary will now be GP in a field at J.14.C.6. (deleted from L)*

NOTE :— While definite sectors are allotted to Units in Reconnaissances 1,2,3, and 4, the M.G.C. wishes as many officers and other ranks as possible to have a general knowledge of all these lines of defence.

It will be noted that in all cases the battle order from right to left is 12th S.L.I., 14th R.H., and 16th Devon Regt.

SECRET   Copy No......18

ADDENDUM to 229th BRIGADE ORDER No.59.
Ref Map Sheet 36A
Scale 1:40,000

1. (a) Lewis Guns will be carried by Units in the Company Lewis Gun Limbers to the Concentration Localities. If, on account of any obstacle, the Lewis Gun Limbers cannot follow immediately in rear of its Company, Lewis Guns and Drums up to the number carried in battle will be immediately issued to the Lewis Gun Sections.

    (b) In the event of the 14th R.H. moving by bus, Lewis Guns and Drums up to the number carried in battle will be taken in the bus. If the unit moves by march route, Lewis Guns and Drums will be carried as laid down in (a) above.

    (c) In the event of 'C' Coy. 74th Battn.M.G.C. moving by bus, Machine Guns and Belt Boxes up to the number taken into battle will be carried in the bus with the personnel of each gun team. If the Unit moves by march route, machine guns and belt boxes will be *Similarly* carried as laid down in (a) above.

2. In moving from present areas to Concentration Localities, ~~16th Devon~~ Regt. will take precedence over ~~12th Som.L.Inf.~~ on the line of march. *16th Devons* / *12 Som L.I.*

3. Reference para. 13 of Brigade Order No.59. 1 Section of 439th Fld. Coy. R.E. having *and* moved to the Asylum at St.VENANT, this Section will receive its order to "Man Battle Stations" from 'C' Coy. 12th S.L.I.

4. On the receipt of the Order "Man Battle Stations", 'B' Teams with the exception of those men detailed for special work in Administrative Instructions to be issued, will proceed to the Divisional Reception Camp.

5. On receipt of the Order "Man Battle Stations". Dress and Equipment will become that laid down in S.S.135, Section XXXI, as near as is possible. Packs will be carried on the man by 16th Devon Regt. and 12th Som.L.Inf. to Concentration Locality ordered where they will be dumped and cleared under orders to be issued by Staff Captain. Units of the Brigade Group in FONTES, will move forward without their packs.
    16th Devon Regt. and 12th Som.L.Inf. will issue 50 Rounds S.A.A. per man on arrival in Concentration Locality, when S.A.A. limbers will be immediately refilled under orders to be issued later. 14th Rl.Highlrs. will carry the extra 50 rounds S.A.A. on the man if the move is by bus. If by march route, the 50 extra rounds S.A.A. will be issued on arrival in Concentration Locality.

6. Reference table attached to Brigade Order No.59, if Units are ordered to take up their allotted Sectors in these lines, Brigade Headquarters will be located as follows :-

    1. BUSNES - STEENBECQUE Line.   Chateau O.36.a.8.8.
       South of LYS Canal.

    2. BUSNES - STEENBECQUE Line.   House   J.30.c.8.4.
       North of LYS Canal.

    3. AMUSOIRES - HAVERSKERQUE - LA MOTTE Line. House P.21.d.2.3.
       South of LYS Canal.

    4. AMUSOIRES - HAVERSKERQUE - LA MOTTE Line. House J.22.c.5.5.
       North of LYS Canal.

    5. LILLERS - STEENBECQUE Line.   MOLINGHEM. O.14.a.central
       South of Canal d'AIRE.

    6. LILLERS - STEENBECQUE Line.   The School, BOESEGHEM,
       North of Canal d'AIRE.   I.8.c.2.2.

7. Administrative Instructions will be issued shortly.

/ 8.

8. ACKNOWLEDGE.

Hd.Qrs. 229th Inf.Bde.
July 2nd 1918.

Captain,
Brigade Major,
229th Infantry Brigade.

Issued at ....

Copies to :-

    No. 1 B.G.C., 229th Infy.Bde.
        2 74th (Yeo) Div.
        3 16th Devon Regt.
3 Copies - 4 12th Som.L.Inf.
        5 14th Rl.Highlrs.
        6 229th L.T.M.Bty.
        7 'C' Coy.74th Bn.M.G.C.
        8 74th Battn.M.G.C.
        9 2 29th Field Amb.
2 Copies 10)
       11) 439th Fld.Coy.R.E.
       12 448th Coy.A.S.C.
To Pass (13 Staff Captain
       14 Brigade Major
To Pass (15 Intelligence Officer
       16 229th Bde.Signal Offr.
       17 War Diary
       18 File
       19 61st Division
       20   5th Division.

SECRET.

REFERENCE ADDENDUM to 229th Brigade Order No.59 para.6 No.2. BUSNES - STEENBECQUE Line N.of LYS Canal.

Ref.Map Sheet 36A
Scale 1:40,000

Brigade Headquarters will be in a House at I.30.c.8.4. and NOT J.30.c.8.4. as stated.

J.M. Tuck
Captain,
Brigade Major,
229th Infantry Brigade.

4-7-18.

Issued to all Recipients of 229th Brigade Order No.59.

SECRET   Copy No. 18

                           ADMINISTRATIVE INSTRUCTIONS
Map Ref.   Issued in Conjunction with 229th Brigade Order
Sheet 36A   No.59 and Addendum.
Scale 1:40,000
-----

1. **Blankets.** Blankets of 16th Devon Regt. 12th Som.L.Inf. (less two Coys) and 1 Section, 439th Fld.Coy. R.E. will be rolled in bundles of ten and left stacked in the vicinity of the present camp, each stack bearing a label stating to what Unit they belong. Those of the 2 detached Coys. of the 12th Som.L.Inf. and 1 section R.E. will be similarly stacked at their present billet. No Guard will be left on them.
Units in FONTES will leave theirs similarly stacked under a Guard of one N.C.O. and three men of the 'B' Teams.
Blankets of the 229th Field Amb. will be left with personnel remaining at LAMBRES.

2. **Water.** Waterbottles will be carried full, and should be filled forthwith and kept full in the case of the 16th Devon Regt. 12th Som.L.Inf. and 2 sections of 439th Fld.Coy. R.E.
Water Carts will be filled before starting. This may not be possible in the case of the above mentioned Units, who will detail an officer to ascertain where they can be filled in the vicinity of the Concentration Point of each area forthwith, and their Water Carts will be filled immediately on arrival there.

3. **Field Kitchens.** These will accompany the transport of each Unit to the Concentration Point.

4. **Packs & Greatcoats.** The Greatcoat will be left in the Pack. O.C., 16th Devon Regt. and 12th Som.L.Inf. will each detail a 'B' Team officer to select one place in the vicinity of each of the 3 Concentration Points, where packs of both units and 2 Sections R.E. can be dumped. It must be borne in mind that the place selected must be accessible to Transport.
A Guard of 1 N.C.O. and 3 men per Unit from the 'B' Teams will be detailed to take charge of this dump.
Men of 'B' Teams will carry their packs to the Divisional Reception Camp at WITTERNESSE.
Units in FONTES will leave their packs with their Blankets.

5. **Rations.** The unexpired portion of the days ration will be carried on the man, one days reserve ration on the ration wagons. Units who are not in possession of one days reserve rations will draw these and their supply wagons at the Supply Dump FONTES immediately on receipt of orders to move.

6. ACKNOWLEDGE.

                                                    Captain,
                                                for Staff Captain,
Hd.Qrs. 229th Inf.Bde.   229th Infantry Brigade.
  2nd July 1918.

     Issued at ..... 7 pm.

     Copies as per Brigade Order No.59.

SECRET

Map Ref. Sheet 36A
Scale 1:40,000.

AMMENDMENT TO BRIGADE ORDER No.59.

1. With the object of preventing congestion in any one part of the three selected "Areas of Concentration", the following fresh allotment of enlarged areas to troops has been made, and those previously allotted in Brigade Order No.59 para.5c. are cancelled except where repeated.

Unit.	Right Locality.	Centre Locality.	Left Locality.
Bde.Hd.Qrs.	House O.28.b.3.4.	House I.31.d.6.8. (at Railway Crossing)	House I.16.a.8.2.
12th S.L.I.	O.36.a.& b.	O.3.a.	I.16.a.
14th R.H.	O.30.a.	(I.31.d. (S.of Railway	I.15.a.
16th Devons	(O.22.d. (O.23.c.	I.31.a.	I.16.b.
'C' Coy.M.G.Bn.	O.35.a.& b.c.	(I.31.d. (W.of Railway.	I.14.b.
L.T.M.Battery	O.34.b.)	)	)
2 Sections 439th Fld.Coy.R.E.	O.28.d.)	O.2.d.8.9.	) I.15.a.
229th Fld.Amb.	O.22.c.	I.32.c.	I.14.a.

Units will not adopt any close formation, but keep under cover of the hedges and trees, so as to be free from Aeroplane Observation.
The Transport of Units similarly will not be parked, but be scattered in covered positions in their allotted areas.

2. A Reconnaissance of these Areas will be made forthwith.

3. ACKNOWLEDGE.

[signature]

Captain,
Brigade Major,
229th Infantry Brigade.

Hd.Qrs. 229th Inf.Bde.
July 3rd 1918.

Issued to all Recipients of Brigade Order No.59.

W.D.

SECRET.

Copy No. 14

229th BRIGADE ORDER No.60

Reference Map
Sheet 36a 1:40,000.

Headquarters,
229th Infantry Bde.

1. The 74th Division will relieve the 61st Division in Right Divisional Sector XI Corps, commencing July 10th.

2. 229th Infantry Brigade will relieve 230th Infantry Brigade in Divisional Reserve concentrated as shown below on July 11th, and come under Orders of G.O.C., 61st Division.

   Headquarters 229th Inf.Bde.   HAM en ARTOIS
   16th Devon Regt.   GUARBECQUE
   12th Som.L.I.   La MIQUELLERIE
   14th Rl.Highlrs.   HAM en ARTOIS
   229th L.T.M.Bty.   HAM en ARTOIS

3. The Command of the Divisional Sector passes from G.O.C.61st Division to G.O.C., 74th Division at 10 a.m. July 14th at which hour 74th Divisional Headquarters closes at MORBECQ FONTES and opens at NCLINGHEM.

4. Details as to relief of Units of 230th Infantry Brigade by Units of the 229th Infantry Brigade and Administrative Instructions will be notified later.

5. The 230th Infantry Brigade will relieve 182nd Infantry Brigade in the Right Brigade Sector on night July 11/12th.
The 231st Infantry Brigade will relieve the 183rd Infantry Brigade in the Left Brigade Sector on night July 10/11th.

6. Completion of all reliefs will be wired or sent by Special Runner to this Headquarters.

7. ACKNOWLEDGE.

Tuck
Captain,
Brigade Major,
229th Infantry Brigade.

July 9th 1918.

Issued at 5 p.m.

Copies to :-

        No.1 B.G.C.,229th Inf.Bde.
          2   16th Devon Regt.
          3   12th Som.L.I.
          4   14th Rl.Highlrs.
          5   229th L.T.M.Bty.
          6   74th (Yeo) Division
          7   230th Infantry Brigade
          8   61st Division
          9   5th Division
         10   Brigade Major
         11   Staff Captain
         12   O.C.,No.2 Sect.Signal Coy.
         13   Intelligence Officer
         14   War Diary
         15   File.

O.C.16th Devons,
O.C.12th Som L.I.

Reference Brigade Order No 60. The Units of the 230th Brigade, who are being relieved tomorrow will not leave their present billets for the line until about 6 or 7. p.m. It will therefore be necessary for Units of this Brigade to share the 230th Billeting area until that hour.

10.7.18.

C. Ju Tuck
Captain,
Brigade Major,
229th Infantry Brigade,

SECRET   Copy No. 15

Reference 229th BRIGADE ORDER No. 60.

Ref. Map   Headquarters,
Sheet 36a. 1:40,000   229th Infantry Bde.

1. 229th Infantry Brigade will relieve the 230th Infantry Brigade in Divisional Reserve tomorrow, July 11th, in accordance with Table overleaf.

2. All Moves will be completed by 11 a.m.

3. Intervals of two hundred yards between platoons will be maintained, and First Line Transport will move in groups of three vehicles each at 100 yards interval.

4. Brigade Headquarters will close at LILETTE at 5 p.m. and reopen at the same hour at HAM en ARTOIS.

5. ACKNOWLEDGE.

                                                Captain,
                                              Brigade Major,
                                           229th Infantry Brigade.

July 10th 1918.

Issued at ...3 a.m...

Copies to :-

    No.1 B.G.C., 229th Inf. Bde.
     2 16th Devon Regt.
     3 12th Som.L.I.
     4 14th Rl.Highlrs.
     5 229th L.T.M.Bty.
     6 74th (Yeo) Division
     7 230th Infantry Brigade
     8 61st Division
     9 5th Division
    10 A.P.M., 74th (Yeo) Div.
    11 Brigade Major
    12 Staff Captain
    13 O.C., No.2 Section Signal Coy.
    14 Intelligence Officer.
    15 War Diary
    16 File.

MARCH TABLE.

Unit.	From.	To.	Relieving.	Route.	Remarks.
16th Devon Regt.	Camp J.25.a.	GUARBECQUE.	16th Sussex.	I.24.central 23.d, 28.d, 31.central, Canal bank to O.12.c.	
12th Som.L.I. (less 2 Coys)	Camp, J.19.c.	LA MOTILERIE	15th Suffolks.	I.30.c & d, I.36, P.2.a, HAUTE BILLET, Canal Bank, to P.20. LA PIERRIERE.	Two coys. at St. VENANT and BUSNES by most direct route.
13th Rl.Highlrs.	FONTES	HAM en ARTOIS.	10th Buffs.	N.30.c.1.9. N.35.b.& d, 36.c, MALAKOY FARM in 31.a, thence to HAM.	Pass Starting Point at N.30.c.1.9. at 8 a.m.
229th L.T.M.Bty.	FONTES	HAM en ARTOIS.	230th L.T.M.Bty.	ditto	Pass Starting Point at N.30.c.1.9. at 8.30 a.m.
H.Q.,229th Bde. and No.2 Sect. Div.Signal Coy.	FONTES	HAM en ARTOIS	H.Q.,230th Bde. and attached Sect.Div.Sig. Coy.	ditto	Will be notified later.

SECRET   Copy No. 14

ADMINISTRATIVE INSTRUCTIONS

Ref.Map
Sheet 36a.   issued in conjunction with Brigade Order No.60.
1:40,000
                                                        Headquarters,
                                                          229th Infantry Bde.

1. **Area Stores.**   A list of any Area Stores taken over in the new area
                           will be sent to this office on the 12th instant.

2. **Rations.**   No Rations will be drawn on the 11th inst.
                           They will be drawn on the 12th inst. for consumption
                           on the 13th inst. at 10 a.m. and thereafter at 7.30 a.m.
                           Refilling Point is MAZINGHEM (N.23.b.)

3. **Supply & Baggage**   After Rations are drawn on 12th inst. Supply and
   Waggons.   Baggage Waggons will be returned to Divisional Train
                           at MAZINGHEM.

4. **Motor Transport.**   Lorries for conveyance of blankets will be provided
                           as follows :-

                               1 per Battn.
                               1 for Bde.Hd.Qrs. and L.T.M.Bty.

                           14th Rl.Highlrs will send a guide for theirs to Bde.
                           Headquarters at 9 a.m.
                           Those for 16th Devon Regt and 12th Som.L.I. will be
                           sent to these Units after being loaded with baggage
                           at the Dump at FONTES. The Staff Captain will arrange
                           this.

5. **Billeting**   These will report at 8 a.m. as follows :-
   Parties.   The Officers must know the ration strength in detail
                           of their units.

                           16th Devon Regt.   to Town Major at GUARBECQUE
                           12th Som.L.I.   to Billet Warden at LA MIQUELLERIE.
                           14th Rl.Highlrs.   to Area Commandant at HAM en ARTOIS.
                           229th L.T.M.Bty.   to Area Commandant at HAM en ARTOIS.

                                                        J M Tuck
                                                        Captain
                                                        for Staff Captain,
                                                        229th Infantry Brigade.

July 10th 1918.
Issued at ....

Copies to :-
            No. 1 B.G.C., 229th Inf.Bde.   No. 10 Brigade Major,
                2 16th Devon Regt.   11 Staff Captain
                3 12th Som.L.I.   12 O.C., No.2 Sect.
                4 14th Rl.Highlrs.   Signal Coy.
                5 229th L.T.M.Bty.   13 Intelligence Off
                6 74th (Yeo) Div.   14 War Diary
                7 61st Division   15 File.
                8 5th Division
                9 230th Infantry Bde.

SECRET.   Copy No. 12

229th BRIGADE ORDER No 61.

Reference Map Sheet
36a.(1/40,000.)

1. Pending further instructions, on receipt of orders to "Man Battle Stations", the Brigade will act as follows while in Divisional reserve:-
   (a) Brigade Headquarters move up to the Headquarters of the left advanced Brigade in O.12.d.
   (b) The three Battalions move from present billets to positions of assembly as under :-
       (i) 12th Somerset L.I. (LA MIQUELLERIE) to O.24.a.
       (ii) 16th Devons. (GUARBECQUE) to P.13.a. North of the Canal and west of the Railway.
       (iii) 14th R.Highlrs.(HAM-EN-ARTOIS) to O.18.a.
   (c) One company of the Machine Gun Battalion also joins the Brigade and has its position of assembly in O.18.a.

2. Units must be prepared to concentrate at the above positions of assembly at short notice, and to move therefrom fully equipped for action. Open formations should be adopted to minimise risk of casualty from shell fire.

3. The Brigade is to be prepared to:-
   (a) Counter attack to regain any portion of the Divisional front system - general line O.20.a. Central to Q.1. Central. Such counter attack would be carried out from a forward assembly position in the AMUSOIRES-HAVERSKERQUE line.
   (b) Form a defensive line on the South along the General line of the N O C River - in the event of the enemy penetrating our front further south, and seizing the HINGES - MT BERNENCHON Ridge.
   (c) Counter attack along the north side of the LYS CANAL, in event of the Division on our left being driven back, while our own Divisional front remained intact.

(4) When Units move out to their positions of assembly all transport, less pack mules, is to be sent back to HAM-EN-ARTOIS and transport Officers will report to the Transport Officer 14th R.Highlrs, who will take steps forthwith to find suitable places W? and S.W. of HAM-EN-ARTOIS for the Brigade Transport to assemble.

5. ACKNOWLEDGE.

Issued at ..11.pm

11.7.18.

Captain,
Brigade Major,
229th Infantry Brigade.

Copies to:-
No. 1. B.G.C.
2. 16th Devons.
3. 12th Somerset L.I.
4. 14th R.Highlrs.
5. 74th M.G.Battn.
6. 61st Division.
7. 74th Division.
8. O.C.No 2 Section.Signals.
9. 231st Brigade.
10. Staff Captain,
11. War Diary.
12. File.
13. Transport Officer, 14th R.Highlrs.
14. Brigade Major,
15. Intelligence Officer.

Reference 229th. Infantry Brigade Order No.61, dated 11-7-18.

In para 3 a. for O.20.a. Central read Q.20.a. Central.

12-7-18.
            Captain,
           Brigade Major,
        229th. Infantry Brigade.

SECRET.   229th INFANTRY BRIGADE ORDER No. 62.   Copy No. 17

Ref. Map, Sheet 36 a.
       1/40,000.

1. The 229th Infantry Brigade will relieve the 230th Infantry Brigade in the ROBECQ Section on the night 23/24th July in accordance with attached table.

2. All details as to guides, times, etc., will be arranged between Commanding Officers concerned, provided that times in attached table are complied with.

3. On July 23rd "B" Teams of the 229th Infantry Brigade will proceed to the Divisional Reception Camp, WITTERNESSE.

4. (a) Defence instructions, aeroplane photographs and special maps will be taken over in the line and receipts given.
   (b) S.A.A., S.O.S. grenades, bombs, area and trench stores, etc., will be taken over in the line and receipts given. A list of stores taken over will be forwarded to this office by 8 p.m. July 24th.

5. In order to assist the 229th Infantry Brigade to become familiar with the Section, the following are being left in the line for an additional 24 hours by the 230th Infantry Brigade:-
   Bde. H.Q. - Intelligence Officer and 3 O.Rs
                Signal Section.
   Each Battn. in line - 1 Officer and 2 N.C.Os with Battn. H.Q.
                         2 N.COs with each Company.

6. (a) The 14th Rl.Highlrs. will arrange to relieve the seven bridge guards shewn below and on map attached by 4 p.m. July 23rd, and will continue to find these guards during the period the Battalion is in Brigade Reserve.

Number of Bridge.	No. of Guards.	At present held by.	Remarks.
44	1	16th Sussex	-
49	1	15th Suffolk	-
51	} 1	do.	-
52		do.	-
53		do.	-
55	1	10th Buffs	-
56	1	do.	-
91	1	16th Sussex	Syphon.
ROBECQ Bridge	1	16th Suffolk	at P.29.b.5.3.

   (b) The reserve Battalion will also reconnoitre Pack Animal Bridges 47, 54, 57 and footbridge 44a.
   (c) These guards will be visited by an Officer of the Battalion by day and by night.

7. The completion of relief by Units will be notified to this H.Q. by use of the following code words:-
          16th Devons   -   Stag
          12tht Som.L.I.   -   Bull
          14th Rl.Highlrs. -   Bear
          229th T.M.B.   -   Unique

8. Command of the ROBECQ Section will pass to B.G.C. 229th Infantry Brigade at 9 a.m. July 24th, at which hour 229th Bde. H.Q. will close at HAM-EN-ARTOIS and re-open at Chateau de BEAULIEU, P.31.c.3.7.

9. Administrative orders for this relief follow.

10. ACKNOWLEDGE.

Issued at 9.a.m.
22-7-18.
                                            Captain,
                                            Brigade Major,
                                            229th Infantry Brigade.

Copies to:-

	1.	B.G.C.
x	2.	16th Devon Regt.
x	3.	14th Rl. Highlrs.
x	4.	12th Som. L.Inf.
	5.	229th T. M. Bty.
	6.	231st Inf. Brigade.
	7.	230th Inf. Brigade.
	8.	74th (Yeo.) Division.
	9.	12th Brigade (4th Division).

Area Commandants -
10. LA MIQUELLERIE.
11. HAM-EN-ARTOIS.
12. GUARBECQUE.
13. Brigade Major.
14. Staff Captain.
15. Intelligence Officer.
16. Brigade Signal Officer.
17. War Diary.
18. File.

(Bridge Map issued only to recipients marked with an "x".)

SECRET.

Table issued with 229th INFANTRY BRIGADE ORDER No. 62.

Serial No.	Unit.	From	To	Relieving	Remarks.
1.	12th Som.L.I.	LA MIQUELLERIE	Right Subsection. H.Q. P.24.d.75.90.	15th Suffolks	Not to cross the AIRE-LA BASSEE Canal before 9.30 p.m.
2.	16th Devons	GUARBECQUE	Left Subsection. H.Q. P.17.b.10.25.	16th Sussex	do.
3.	14th R.Highlrs.	HAM-EN-ARTOIS	LA PIERRIERE In Brigade Reserve	10th Buffs.	Not to reach LA PIERRIERE before 9.30 p.m.
4.	229th T.M.Bty.	HAM-EN-ARTOIS		230th T.M.Bty.	

NOTE: Distances of 100 yards will be maintained between Platoons marching forward.

SECRET.

ADMINISTRATIVE INSTRUCTIONS
relative to
229th INFANTRY BRIGADE ORDER No. 62.

1. **Trench and Area Stores.**
    Each Unit will take over all trench and area stores in the area of the Unit of the 230th Brigade which they relieve. A list of these will be forwarded to reach this office by 8 p.m. on 24th inst.

2. **Ammunition and Supply Dumps.**
    Each Unit will take over from their corresponding Unit of the 230th Brigade all ammunition, reserve ration, and water dumps within their sector.
    A list showing the composition and location of these dumps as taken over will be sent to this office by 8 p.m. on 24th inst.

3. **Baggage Wagons.**
    2 baggage wagons for each Infantry Battalion will report at the respective Battalion Headquarters at 10 a.m. to-morrow, 23rd inst.

4. **Motor Lorries.**
    One Motor Lorry will report at the Headquarters of each Battalion at 9 a.m. on 23rd inst. to convey blankets, etc. of "B" Teams to WITTERNESSE. The 14th Rl. Highlrs. lorry will also take "B" Team baggage of 229th T. M. Bty. O.C. 229th T. M. Bty. will arrange for all his "B" Team baggage to be at 14th Rl. Highlrs. Headquarters by 8.30 a.m. to-morrow, 23rd inst.

5. **Transport Lines, etc.**
    Each Unit will send their transport and Quartermaster's stores to MOLINGHEM on 23rd inst., taking over the billets and transport lines at present occupied by their corresponding Unit of the 230th Brigade.
    Blankets and Officers valises of Battalions going into the line will be sent to MOLINGHEM to-morrow, - those of the Battalion in reserve may be taken with them to LA PIERRIERE if so desired.

6. **Supplies.**
    Refilling point will remain at FONTES. Representatives of Units will be at the Dump at 8 a.m. each morning from and including 24th inst., to take over their rations. These will be delivered by train transport to each Unit's Q.M's stores at MOLINGHEM and will be sent on from there by 1st Line Transport. The 229th T. M. Bty. supplies will be sent from MOLINGHEM on the Brigade Headquarters limber to Brigade Headquarters, and will then be delivered under Brigade arrangements to the T.M.B. Headquarters each night.

7. **Exchange of S.A.A.**
    Each Battalion will leave 64 full boxes S.A.A. in their present areas, and will find a corresponding amount in the transport lines which they take over at MOLINGHEM.

                                            Captain,
                                            Staff Captain,
                                            229th Infantry Brigade.

22-7-18.

Copies to :-   16th Devon Regt.   229th T.M.Bty.
                12th Som.L.Inf.   Brigade Major.
                14th Rl. Highlrs.

SECRET

Copy No...... 15

229th BRIGADE ORDER No.63.

Headquarters,
229th Inf. Bde.

1. The 14th R.H. will relieve the 12th Som.L.I. in the Right Sub-sector of the ROBECQ Sector the night of July 31st/ August 1st.

2. All details of relief will be arranged by Commanding Officers concerned.

3. In order to help 14th R.H. become familiar with the line the following will be left in the line by O.C., 12th Som. L.I. for twenty-four hours :-
   1 Officer from Battn. Headquarters
   2 N.C.O's per Company, except company in Front Line Posts who will leave one N.C.O. per post.

4. No forward movement will take place by 14th R.H. East of LA BASSEE Canal before 9.15 p.m.

5. (a) All ammunition, rations and water dumps, all trench and area stores including aeroplane photographs and special maps of the sector will be handed over to incoming Units, receipts being given and taken.
   (b) A list of all the above will be sent by incoming and outgoing Units to Brigade Headquarters by 8 p.m. August 1st.

6. Great care should be taken by Commanding Officers and Company Commanders to hand over all possible information regarding Patrols or intended Raids.

7. Completion of Relief will be wired to Brigade Headquarters by use of code word "CLARENCE".

8. First Line Transport of Units will not move from their present lines.

9. ACKNOWLEDGE.

Captain,
Brigade Major,
229th Infantry Brigade.

July 30th 1918.

Issued at ....

Copies to :-

No.1 B.G.C., 229th Infy. Bde.
  2 16th Devon Regt.
  3 12th Som.L.I.
  4 14th Rl.Highlrs.
  5 Hd.Qrs. 74th (Yeo) Div.
  6   "   "   231st Brigade
  7   "   "   10th Brigade
  8   "   "   44th Brigade R.F.A.
  9 Right Group M.G.Battn.
 10 No.5 R.M.R.E.
 11 229th L.T.M.Batty.
 12 Staff Captain
 13 Brigade Major
 14 War Diary
 15 File.

Vol 5.

Headquarters,
229th Inf. Bde.
(74th Division)

August 918.

Headquarters,

74th. Yeo. Division.

Herewith War Diary for the month of August 1918, for 229th. Infantry Brigade H.Q.

for B.G.C. Captain, Brigade Major,
229th. Infantry Brigade,

Map Ref:
Sheet HAZEBROUCK Sa 1/100,000
36a 1/40,000

Instructions regarding War Diaries and Intelligence
Summaries are contained in F.S. Regs., Part II.
and the Staff Manual respectively. Title pages
will be prepared in manuscript.

WAR DIARY
or
INTELLIGENCE SUMMARY.
(Erase heading not required.)

Army Form C. 2118.

WO 5

Po 8 1. HQ 229 Inf Bde

Place	Date	Hour	Summary of Events and Information	Remarks and references to Appendices
BUSNES	Night 5/6 August		Enemy showing signs of withdrawal. 14 R.H. and 2 Devons advance to follow up enemy on their own initiative. Enemy front line occupied during the night.	
CARVIN	6		Bde. H.Q. moved to CARVIN.	
	13/14		Between these dates the Brigade further the enemy back to the line of the TURBAUTE stream. Limited objectives were laid down and all went according to plan. The Somersets relieved the Devons on night 8/9. On night 13/14 2/30th Brigade Bde Relieved to fall S. and took over line from 229th Brigade. Units returned to the AMUSORES - HAVERSKERQUE - Supplus area as before.	
LABIETTE FARM	14		H.Q. opened at Plum.	
Haverskerque ART.	16/17		Units moved to a new area as shewn in Brigade Order No 66 attached.	
"	29/23		74th Division extended its front to the South in accordance with Brigade Order No 67 attached.	

Army Form C. 2118.

WAR DIARY
or
INTELLIGENCE SUMMARY.

(Erase heading not required.)

Page 4

Place	Date August	Hour	Summary of Events and Information	Remarks and references to Appendices
HAM en ARTOIS	24/25		229 Brigade relieved the 231 Brigade in the line in accordance with Brigade Order No 68 attached.	
Q19a.6.7	27/8/16		229 Brigade was relieved by the 177 (59th Division) Brigade in accordance with Brigade Order No 69 attached and moved to to HAM en ARTOIS area.	
HAM en ARTOIS	26/27.28.		229 Brigade entrained at BERGUETTE for CORBIE. Arrived in FRANVILLERS and a Mousseure. Brigade H.Q. at Q Chateau at BEHENCOURT.	
BEHENCOURT	29.		Reconnoitred after area.	
	30		Brigade moved by bus to MARICOURT.	
	31		Brigade bussed and entrained in area between MAUREPAS and Marched to and Bivouaked. Brigade H.Q. at T.26.d.9.5. CHERY sur SOMME. Brigade references are Amiens Sheet 1/100,000 and Note: after ninety from map references are Amiens Sheet 62.c. Scale 1/40,000.	
T.26.d.9.5 or 15/11/16		B.E.F.		

A.J.M. Tuck
Captain
Brigade Major

SECRET FILE   Copy No. 15

229th BRIGADE ORDER No. 64.

Headquarters,
229th Infantry Brigade.

1. The 12th Som.L.I. will relieve the 16th Devon Regt. in the Left Sub-sector of the ROBECQ Sector the night of August 8th/9th.

2. All details of relief will be arranged by Commanding Officers concerned.

3. In order to help the 12th Som.L.I. to become familiar with the line, the following will be left in the line by O.C., 16th Devon Regt. for twenty-four hours :-
    1 Officer from Battn. Headquarters.
    2 N.C.O's per Company, except companies in Front Line Posts who will leave one N.C.O. per platoon.

4. No forward movement will take place by 12th Som.L.I. East of LA BASSEE Canal before 9.15 p.m.

5. (a) All ammunition, rations and water dumps, all trench and area stores including aeroplane photographs and special maps of the sector will be handed over to incoming Units, receipts being given and taken.
   (b) A list of all the above will be sent by incoming and outgoing Units to Brigade Headquarters by 10 p.m. August 9th.

6. Great care should be taken by Commanding Officers and Company Commanders to hand over all possible information regarding Patrols or intended Raids.

7. Completion of Relief will be wired to Brigade Headquarters by use of code word "NOC".

8. First Line Transport of Units will not move from their present lines.

9. (a) All extra-regimental guards (including bridge-guards) found by the 12th Som.L.I., will be relieved by the 16th Devon Regt. by 5 p.m. August 8th. Written orders will be handed over by Officer i/c Bridge-Guards and by each Bridge Guard in accordance with Defence Scheme Appendix "A", paras. 2 and 3.
   (b) All details for working parties of Battn. in Brigade Reserve will be handed over by 12th Som.L.I. to 16th Devon Regt.

10. ACKNOWLEDGE.

August 6th 1918.

Issued at ...7 p.m.

Captain,
Brigade Major,
229th Infantry Brigade.

Copies to :-

    No.1 B.G.C., 229th Infy. Bde.
    2   16th Devon Regt.
    3   12th Som.L.I.
    4   14th Bl.Highlrs.
    5   Hd.Qrs. 74th (Yeo) Div.
    6   "   "   231st Brigade
    7   "   "   10th Brigade
    8   "   "   44th Brigade R.F.A.
    9   Right Group M.G. Battn.
    10 No.5 R.M.R.E.
    11 229th L.T.M. Batty.
    12 Staff Captain,
    13 Brigade Major,
    14 War Diary,
    15 File.

SECRET

229th BRIGADE ORDER No. 65.

Copy No. 16

10th August 1918.

1. The enemy's position along the right bank of the BOURRE River and thence Southwards to the MERVILLE-PARADIS Road appears to be well organised and held in some strength, probably with the object of covering the completion of a more permanent line which has been located by aeroplane photographs and extends from the West side of NEUF BERQUIN through L.13,19,25 to 31 and thence West of LESTREM and the LAWE.

2. The further progress of the 74th Division depends upon the progress made by the two flank Divisions. The present front line will be organised as a strong outpost position. Patrolling will be very active and every endeavour will be made to discover any weakening of the enemy's defence.

3. The Division will be organized in depth.
    The 15th Suffolks will relieve the 229th Brigade Group on the night 10th/11th August, who will take over the Reserve Line and AMUSOIRES System and be disposed in depth as follows :-

    16th Devon Regt. in the Reserve Line and Front and Support Lines of the AMUSOIRES and HAVERSKERQUE Line of the St. FLORIS Sector.

    12th Som.L.I. in the Reserve Line and Front and Support Lines of the AMUSOIRES and HAVERSKERQUE Line of the ROBECQ Sector.

    14th Rl.Highlrs. in Brigade Reserve in the Reserve Line of the AMUSOIRES and HAVERSKERQUE Line in both St. FLORIS and ROBECQ Sectors.

    229th L.T.M.Bty. will leave two Stokes Mortars in line under arrangements to be made with O.C., 230th L.T.M.Bty. direct.

4. Headquarters, 229th Brigade, LABIETTE FARM.
    Headquarters of Units will be notified later.
    R.M.Field Coy.R.E. and detachment of the Field Ambulance attached to 229th Brigade Group will revert to the Command of the C.R.E. and A.D.M.S. respectively.

5. All details of the Relief of 12th Som.L.I. and 14th Rl.Highlrs. will be arranged with O.C., 15th Suffolks direct.

6. Administrative Arrangements for the relief are being arranged by Staff Captain and Rear Battn. Headquarters direct.

7. Headquarters, 229th Brigade will close at CARVIN on completion of Relief and re-open at LABIETTE FARM on arrival.

8. Relief complete will be wired to Brigade Headquarters by code word, The Code Word will be the name of the Commanding Officer concerned.

9. ACKNOWLEDGE.

Issued at 5 pm

Captain,
Brigade Major,
229th Infantry Brigade.

Copies to :-
No. 1 O.C., 229th Brigade,
2 O.C., 16th Devon Regt.
3 O.C., 12th Som.L.I.
4 O.C., 14th Rl.Highlrs.
5 O.C., 229th L.T.M.Bty.
6 O.C., 5th R.M.R.E.
7 O.C., 'C' Coy.M.G.Bn.
8 H.Q., 44th Bde.R.F.A.
No. 9 H.Q., 230th Brigade
10 H.Q., 11th Brigade,
11 H.Q., 74th Division
12 Bde. Signal Offr.
13 Staff Captain
14 Brigade Major,
15 War Diary,
16 File.

SECRET. W.D   Copy No. 17

229th INFANTRY BRIGADE ORDER No. 66.

H.Q., 229th Inf. Bde.
15th Aug. 1918.

1. The 231st Brigade will relieve 230th Brigade in the line on the night August 16/17th.

2. On the same night 230th Brigade will take over responsibility for the Reserve Line and 229th Brigade will move into Divisional Reserve and be located as follows :-

Brigade Hd.Qrs.	...	HAM en ARTOIS.
16th Devon Regt.	...	HAM en ARTOIS.
12th Som.L.I.	...	GUARBECQUE.
14th Rl. Highlrs.	...	La MIQUELLERIE.
229th L.T.M. Batty.	...	HAM en ARTOIS.

3. "C" Coy. M.G. Battn. now attached to 229th Brigade will come under orders of 230th Brigade.

4. The two guns of the 229th L.T.M. Batty. now in line will be relieved by two guns of the 230th L.T.M. Batty. Details to be arranged between O.Cs. L.T.M. Batteries concerned.

5. O.C., 16th Devons will hand over to O.C., 10th Buffs, and O.C., 12th Som.L.I. will hand over to O.C., 15th Suffolks all information concerning areas now occupied, defence instructions, details of work, trench stores etc. Receipts for trench or area stores handed over should be sent to this Headquarters by 3 p.m. Aug 17th

6. The locations shewn in para. 2 above should be reconnoitred forthwith, with a view to finding parade grounds, 30 yards ranges, etc. Os.C. Units will get in touch with Os.C. whose Units were previously located in the same Villages.

7. (a) "B" Teams TRANSPORT LINES of will rejoin their Units on August 15th.
   (b) Administrative Orders for move of this Brigade will be notified by Staff Captain.

8. Completion of move from present to new areas will be wired or sent by bicycle orderly to Brigade Headquarters immediately upon arrival. Code Word will be name of Commanding Officer concerned.

9. The time of the closing of Brigade Headquarters will be notified later.

10. ACKNOWLEDGE.

Captain,
Brigade Major,
229th Infantry Brigade.

Issued at 5 p.m.

Copies to :-

No. 1.	O.C., 229th Inf. Bde.	10.	74th (Yeo) Division,
2.	O.C., 16th Devon Regt.	11.	443th Coy. A.S.C.
3.	O.C., 12th Som.L.I.	12.	Sub Area Commdt. HAM en ARTOIS.
4.	O.C., 14th Rl. Highlrs.	13.	" " " GUARBECQUE.
5.	O.C., 229th L.T.M. Bty.	14	Staff Captain.
6.	O.C., 'C' Coy.M.G.Bn.	15	Brigade Signalling Officer
7.	O.C., 5th R.M.R.E.	16	Brigade Major.
8.	230th Infantry Bde.	17	War Diary.
9.	231st Infantry Bde.	18	File.

W.D

SECRET

ADDENDA TO 229th INFANTRY BRIGADE ORDER No.66.

Hd.Qrs. 229th Inf.Bde.
August 15th 1918.

1. Brigade Headquarters will close at LABIETTE FARM at 9.30 p.m. on 16th instant, and reopen at HAM-en-ARTOIS on arrival.

2. The two guns of the 229th L.T.M.Batty. will be relieved by two guns of the 231st L.T.M.Batty. and not by the 230th L.T.M.Batty. as stated.

3. When the tail of Units of the 231st Brigade have passed the Reserve Line, Units of the 229th Brigade may move to their new areas without waiting for the arrival of Units of 230th Brigade from the line.
Units of the 231st Brigade have orders not to cross the road running through LES AMUSOIRES and Squares F.11,17, and 23 before 9 p.m., and are using roads and tracks running W. and E. through F.5, F.%, and F.29.

4. 'B' Teams will move on August 16th to Villages where their Units are to be billeted, and not to present transport lines.

C Mackintosh
Captain,
for Brigade Major,
229th Infantry Brigade.

Copies to :-

        O.C., 229th Infantry Brigade,
        O.C., 16th Devon Regt.
        O.C., 12th Som.L.I.
        O.C., 14th Rl.Highlrs.
        O.C., 229th L.T.M.Bty.
        230th Infantry Brigade
        231st Infantry Brigade
        74th (Yeomanry) Division.
        Staff Captain,
        Brigade Signalling Officer,
        War Diary,
        File.

SECRET   Copy No. 6

229th INFANTRY BRIGADE ORDER No. 67.

22nd August 1918.

1. The 74th Division will extend its front on the night 22/23rd August to the South grid line of map squares Q.23, Q.24, R.19, R.20, etc. Eastwards.
    The Divisional Southern Boundary will then run as shown on attached map.

2. The 231st Infantry Brigade will take over the Outpost System as far South as this new boundary and Command of this portion of the Divisional Front passes to G.O.C., 74th Division on completion of the Infantry Relief.

3. (a) 230th Infantry Brigade will take over responsibility for the Reserve Line as far South as the new Divisional Boundary.

    (b) The Reserve Line will be held by a series of nucleus garrisons, consisting of 4 platoons in each Battalion Sector. The remainder of the two Battalions now in the Reserve and AMUSOIRES lines will be billeted in ROBECQ and St. FLORIS.

4. ACKNOWLEDGE.

Issued at ...5 p.m...

                                          Captain,
                                       Brigade Major,
                                    229th Infantry Brigade.

Copies to :-

    No. 1 O.C., 229th Brigade
  x   2 O.C., 16th Devon Regt.
  x   3 O.C., 12th Som.L.I.
  x   4 O.C., 14th Rl.Highlrs.
      5 O.C., 229th L.T.M.Batty.
      6 War Diary,
      7 File.

Maps issued to recipients marked - x

LESTREM

Divisional Boundaries.
Front Line Aug 20th

Scale 1:10,000

SECRET

Copy No. 8...

229th INFANTRY BRIGADE ORDER No.68

August 23rd 1918.

Reference Map 1:40,000. Sheet 36 a.

1. The 229th Infantry Brigade will relieve the 231st Infantry Brigade as Advanced Brigade on the night 24/25th August, in accordance with March Table attached.

2. Forward moves will be carried out in two stages :-
    (a) To Staging Areas.
    (b) To Relief.

3. (a) All details as to Guides, Times etc. will be arranged between Commanding Officers concerned.
   (b) Defence Schemes, Aeroplane Photographs, and Special Maps will be taken over and receipts given.

4. "B" Teams will move to Divisional Reception Camp, LINGHEM on 24th August.

5. 117th Brigade, R.F.A., 439th Field Coy. R.E., "D" Coy. 74th M.G.Battn. and 1 Coy. 11th Cyclist Battalion, at present attached to 231st Infantry Brigade, will come under the orders of B.G.C., 229th Infantry Brigade, when Change of Command passes from B.G.C., 231st Infantry Brigade.

6. The Command of the Advanced Brigade Area will pass to B.G.C., 229th Infantry Brigade at 9.30 a.m. 25th August, at which hour Brigade Headquarters close at HAM-en-ARTOIS, and open simultaneously at Q.19.a.6.7.

7. Completion of Reliefs will be wired Priority to Brigade Headquarters in code - The Code Words will be the names of the Commanding Officers concerned.

8. Administrative Instructions will be issued separately.

9. ACKNOWLEDGE.

Issued at 4.30 P.M.

A. J. M. Tuck.
Captain,
Brigade Major,
229th Infantry Brigade.

Copies to :-

No.1	B.G.C., 229th Inf. Bde.	No.12 439 Fld.Coy.R.E.
2	16th Devon Regt.	13 74th M.G.Battn.
3	12th Som.L.I.	14 O.C., Coy.11th Cyclist Bn.
4	14th Rl.Highlrs.	15 Sub Area Comdt. HAM.
5	230th Inf Brigade	16 " " " GUARBECQUE
6	231st Inf. Brigade	17 Supply Officer
7	183rd Inf Brigade	18 Staff Captain
8	58th Inf. Brigade	19 O.C., No.2 Sect.74th Div. Signal Coy.
9	74th Division.	20 Intelligence Offr. 229th Inf.Bde.
10	229th L.T.M.Batty.	21 File
11	117th Brigade R.F.A.	22 War Diary

SECRET

Copy No. ......

MARCH TABLE.

Issued with Brigade Order No. ....

Serial No.	Unit.	From.	To.	Staging Area.	To Relieve.	Leave Billets.	Route.	Remarks.
1	16th Bn. Devon Regt.	HAM en ARTOIS.	Left Sector.	ASYLUM, St. VENANT.	10th Bn. Kings Shropshire L.I.	9 a.m.	LA MIQUELLERIE - LA PIERRIERE - L'EPINETTE.	
2	12th Bn. Som. L.I.	GUARBECQUE.	Right Sector.		24th Bn. Welsh Regiment.	8 a.m.	Canal Bank Bridge In F.27.a. 8.8. thence ROBECQ.	
3	14th Bn. Rl. Highlrs.	LA MIQUELLERIE.	Brigade Support.	AMUSOIRES System from LES AMUSOIRES to ROBECQ.	25th Bn. Royal Welsh Fus.	9½ a.m.	BUSNES - LA BRASSERIE.	
4	229th L. T.M. Batty.	HAM en ARTOIS.	Line.	ROBECQ.	231st L.T.M. Battery.	9½ a.m.	LA MIQUELLERIE - BUSNES - ROBECQ.	

NOTE :- No Movement East of the Reserve Line will take place before 9.15 p.m.

SECRET

ADMINISTRATIVE INSTRUCTIONS
relative to Brigade Order No. 68.

Trench & Area Stores - Units will take over from their corresponding Unit of the 231st Infantry Brigade all Trench and Area Stores in their possession, including Packsaddles, Message Carrying Rockets, Hot Food Containers and all Solidified Alcohol. Lists of all stores so taken over will be forwarded to reach this office by 6 p.m. on 25th instant. Special care will be taken that units returns include articles taken over in their Transport Lines as well as those in the line.

Ammunition & Supply Dumps - Units will take over from their corresponding Unit of the 231st Infantry Brigade all Ammunition and Supply Dumps in their respective areas. Statements showing the location and composition of these dumps will be forwarded to this office by 6 p.m. on 25th instant.

Supplies -
(a) Rations for consumption 25th will be delivered by train transport tomorrow forenoon, 24th instant, to Asylum St.VENANT for 16th Devons and to ROBECQ for 12th Som.L.I., 14th Rl.Highlrs. and 229th L.T.M.Bty.
(b) From and including 25th instant, rations will be drawn from BUSNES, P.32.a.5.3. at 6.30 a.m. and delivered by train transport to Units Transport lines.

Transport -
(a) Location of transport lines will be as follows :-
Brigade Headquarters   P.24.central
16th Devon Regt.   )
14th Rl.Highlrs.   )   P.6.c.
12th Som.L.I.   P.24.c.9.9.
(b) One G.S.wagon will report to O.C.,229th L.T.M.Batty. at 8 a.m.tomorrow 24th and will be at his disposal all day but must be returned to present Brigade Headquarters on evening of 24th.
(c) One Motor Lorry will report to each of 16th Devons, 12th Som.L.I. and 14th Rl.Highlrs. at 9.30 a.m. tomorrow 24th instant, to convey officers valises and blankets of "B" Teams to Divisional Reception Camp. O.C.,229th L.T.M.Battery will arrange for his "B" Teams baggage to be at 16th Devon Headquarters by 9.15 a.m. tomorrow 24th instant.
(d) All Baggage Wagons must be returned to the Coy.of the Train on the morning of 25th instant.

Salvage - The Main Salvage Dump will be moved from MOLINGHEM to BUSNES on 24th instant. Units will send back Salvage in the ration limbers to their transport lines, where it will be loaded on to the returning supply wagons and taken to the Dump at BUSNES.

23-8-18.

Captain,
Staff Captain,
229th Infantry Brigade.

SECRET.

W.D

Copy No. 16

229th INFANTRY BRIGADE ORDER No.69.

August 26th 1918.

1. The 74th Division will be relieved in the present sector by the 59th Division.

2. The 229th Infantry Brigade will be relieved by the 177th Infantry Brigade on the night 27/28th August, and will move by march route and bus to billeting area in accordance with attached table.

3. All details as to Guides, Time, etc. will be arranged by Commanding Officers concerned.

4. All Special Maps, Aeroplane Photographs and Defence Schemes will be handed over and receipts taken.

5. The Command of the Advanced Brigade Area will pass to B.G.C., 177th Infantry Brigade on completion of relief, at which time Brigade Headquarters will close at Q.19.a.6.7. and will reopen simultaneously at HAM-EN-ARTOIS.

6. O's.C., 16th Devons and 12th Som.L.I. will each detail one Officer (provided with bicycle) to report to Brigade Headquarters at 5.30 p.m. on 27th instant. These Officers will be placed in charge of Embussing Points.

7. Administrative Instructions will be issued separately.

8. One Company, 11th Cyclist Battalion remain in line and will come under orders of B.G.C., 177th Infantry Brigade on completion of relief.

9. Completion of Relief will be wired Priority to Brigade Headquarters using the following Code Names :-
    16th Devons .... FISH   14th Rl.Highlrs .... FOWL
    12th Som.L.I. ...... FLESH   229th L.T.M.Bty .... FEATHER

10. ACKNOWLEDGE.

Issued at 8-30 p.m.

Captain,
Brigade Major,
229th Infantry Brigade.

Copies to :-
    No. 1 B.G.C., 229th Inf.Bde.
        2 O.C., 16th Devon Regt.
        3 O.C., 12th Som.L.I.
        4 O.C., 14th Rl.Highlrs.
        5 O.C., 229th L.T.M.Bty.
        6 74th (Yeomanry) Division.
        7 177th Infantry Brigade
        8 184th   "   "
        9 58th   "   "
       10 O.C., Coy, 11th Cyclist Bn.
       11 O.C., 439th Field Coy. R.E.
       12 Area Commandant, HAM-en-ARTOIS.
       13   "   "   GUARBECQUE.
       14 Staff Captain,
       15 Brigade Signalling Officer,
       16 War Diary.
       17 File.

TABLE.

Serial No.	Unit.	Relieved by	Embussing Point. (Head of Column)	To.	Remarks.
1.	16th Devon Regt.	15th Essex.	P.9.b.8.9.	HAM-on-ARTOIS.	
2.	12th Som.L.I.	11th Com.L.I.	P.23.c.8.3.	MANQUEVILLE	
3.	14th Rl.Highlrs.	2/6th Durham L.I.	P.9.b.8.9.	MOLINGHEM.	
4.	229th L.T.T.Battery	177th L.T.M.Battery		HAM-on-ARTOIS.	
5.	439th Fld.Coy.R.E.	470th Coy. R.E.		BERGUETTE.	

SECRET

ADMINISTRATIVE INSTRUCTIONS
Relative to 229th Brigade Order No.69.

1. **Trench & Area Stores**

    All Trench, Area and R.E.Stores, and all Ammunition Dumps will be handed over to relieving Units. Receipts will be obtained in each case. List of all stores and ammunition handed over will be forwarded to this office.

2. **Tents & Shelters**

    All tents and shelters in possession must be handed over to incoming units. Receipts will be taken for these and units will report to this office number handed over.

3. **Ammunition.**

    First Line Transport will move out with its complete complement of S.A.A. and tools.

4. **Supplies.**

    (a) Rations for consumption 28th will be drawn by representatives of units on train transport at 7 a.m. on 27th at HAM-EN-ARTOIS. These rations will be dumped in area where units will be billeted for night 27/28th and will be issued on the arrival of troops and carried on the man.

    (b) Rations for consumption 29th will be drawn on the same wagons as in (a) at 5 p.m. at HAM-EN-ARTOIS on 27th inst. The wagons will be taken back to units areas and will remain loaded with units and entrain with them on 28th inst.

5. **Transport.**

    (a) Baggage Wagons will report at Units Transport Lines at 4 p.m. today.

    (b) 1 Motor Lorry for each Bn. and 1 for T.M.Battery will be on road beside ROBECQ GHQ/HUTRY at 9 a.m. tomorrow 27 Units will send guides to take their motor lorry over there at that hour and guide it to their Transport Lines.

6. **Reception Camp Details.**

    All 'B' Teams and other details at Reception Camp will join Units on 27th instant.
    Units will send guides to Reception Camp to report there by 10 a.m. on 27th to guide details to the area where their respective units will be billeted for night 27/28th inst.

    OC Reception Camp has been informed of location of units on night 27/28th & transport has been arranged.

7. **Billeting Arrangements**

    Units will send forward a Billeting Party tomorrow morning 27th inst to their billeting areas to ensure that billets are ready before arrival of the troops.

8. **Agriculture**

    Lieuts HAWKINS and DOLLIMORE will remain in this area until harvest is completed. All other personnel of this Brigade at present working at the harvest will be sent to rejoin units tomorrow 27th instant.

/9.

9. **Medical.**

Until arrival in new billeting area units will evacuate sick under existing arrangements. After arrival, they will be evacuated through 229th Field Ambulance at O.31.a.central MALANOY FARM.

26-8-18.

Captain,
Staff Captain,
229th Infantry Brigade.

SECRET

229th INFANTRY BRIGADE GROUP.

ENTRAINING ORDERS.

1. The 229th Infantry Brigade Group will entrain at BERGUETTE in accordance with the attached table.

2. O.C., 16th Devons will detail one Company to load all trains of the Group. This Coy. will be at the Station by 20.00 on 28th and will entrain with its cooker and team by train departing at 20.30 on 29th instant.

3. O.C., 14th R.H. will detail 1 Coy. under Capt. STEWART to offload all trains of this group at Station of destination. This Coy. with its cooker and team will entrain by first train departing 23.30 on 28th instant.

4. Capt. H.A. BLUNT, Sussex Yeo. will act as Div. Entraining Officer at BERGUETTE. Capt. R.W. STEWART, Fife & Forfar Yeo attd. 14th R.H. will act as Divisional Detraining Officer and will wire to 74th Division state of detrainment in accordance with G.R.O.4743 of 11/8/18. He will receive instructions from the A/D.A.A.G., 74th Division.

5. Advance Parties as under will proceed by first train departing at 23.30 on 28th instant.
   Each Inf. Bn.) 1 Officer, 4 C.Q.M.S's, 1 representative of
   & M.G. Bn.   ) Batt. Headquarters, 1 Batman.
   439th Fld. Co.) 1 Officer, 1 Sergeant, 1 Batman.
   229th Fld. Amb)   "   "   "
   448th Coy. A.S.C. - Supply Officer, 1 Sergeant and Batman.
   1 Bicycle will be taken by each officer.

6. Refilling Point on 28th inst. for all 229th Brigade Group including ½ S.A.A. Section 74th D.A.C. HAM-EN-ARTOIS at 2 p.m. Units will send their Supply Wagons to draw at that hour. Rations for consumption 29th will be carried on the man, rations for consumption 30th will be carried on the Supply Wagons except in the case of Units entraining after 12 noon on 29th who will carry the breakfast portion of the ration for 30th on the man.

7. All transport including Baggage and Supply Wagons attached from Div. Train will entrain on same train as H.Q. of Units except in the case of Cookers and teams shown in attached schedule as entraining with detached Coys. Water Carts will be entrained full.

8. Motor Lorries - One Motor Lorry will be provided for each of the 3 Inf. Bns M.G. Bn. 229th Field Amb. and L.T.M. Battery to convey extra baggage by road to destination.
   These Units will send a guide to be at Brigade Headquarters HAM-EN-ARTOIS at 2.30 p.m. today 29th instant to get their lorry. Lorries will be loaded up this afternoon and will rendezvous at 8 p.m. at the Church, HAM-EN-ARTOIS, and will park for the night on the road there under charge of an officer to be detailed by O.C., 12th S.L.I. The lorries will then proceed by road to CORBIE Station under charge of this officer and will there wait further instructions.

9. All horse transport entraining must be at the station 3 hours before departure of train. All personnel entraining must be at the station 1 hour before departure of train. Animals should be watered immediately prior to entrainment.

10. Entraining states for each unit or part of unit entraining must be handed to R.T.O., BERGUETTE, 3 hours before the train carrying each unit or part of unit is due to depart.
    Entraining states must show numbers of officers, men, animals by classes, 4 wheeled and 2 wheeled vehicles, and bicycles entraining on each train. Limbered G.S. Wagons will be shown as 2 wheeled vehicles.

- 2 -

11. Station of detrainment will be CORBIE.

12. ACKNOWLEDGE.

                                                C Mackintosh

                                                   Captain,
                                                Staff Captain,
Issued at 10.30 a.m.   229th Infantry Brigade.
       28/8/18.

    Copies to :-

        16th Devon Regt.
        12th Som.L.I.
        14th Rl.Highlrs.
        74th M.G.Bn.
        229th Field Amb.
        439th Field Coy.R.E.
        448th Coy. A.S.C.
        229th L.T.M.Battery
        S.A.A.Section, 74th D.A.C.
        O.C., 229th Brigade Signals
        File.

229th INFANTRY BRIGADE GROUP.

ENTRAINING STATION BERGUETTE.

Train No.	Hour of Depart.	Date.	Contents.
2	23.30	28/8/18.	229th Bde.H.Q., 229th L.T.M.B., 229th Sig. Section, 229th Field Amb., 1 Coy, Cooker and Team of 14th Bn.R.H. - Advance Party of 229th Bde.Group.
5	2.30	29/8/18.	14th Bn.R.H., less 1 Coy. Cooker and Team.
8	5.30	29/8/18.	12th Bn.Somerset L.I. less 1 Coy. Cooker and Team.
11.	8.30	29/8/18.	16th Bn.Devon Regt. less 1 Coy. Cooker and Team.
14.	11.30	29/8/18.	74th M.G.Bn.H.Q., and 2 Coys.
17.	14.30	29/8/18.	2 Coys. 74th M.G.Battn.
20.	17.30	29/8/18.	439th Fld.Coy.R.E., 448th Coy.Div.Train. 1 Coy., Cooker and Team of 12th Bn.S.L.I.
23.	20.30	29/8/18.	½ S.A.A.Section 74th D.A.C., 1 Coy., Cooker and Team of 16th Bn.Devon Regt.

Composition of Trains :- 1 Coach, 30 Covered\s, 17 Flats.
Transport to be at Station 3 hours before departure of train, personnel 1 hour.

Vol. 6.

Headquarters,
229th Inf. Bde.
(74th Division)

September 1918.

Army Form C. 2118.

WAR DIARY
or
INTELLIGENCE SUMMARY
(Erase heading not required.)

Map Reference Sheet 62c. Scale 1/40,000.
Instructions regarding War Diaries and Intelligence Summaries are contained in F.S. Regs., Part II. and the Staff Manual respectively. Title pages will be prepared in manuscript.

Place	Date	Hour	Summary of Events and Information	Remarks and references to Appendices
	SEPTEMBER 1918.			
	Night Sept. 1/2nd.		229th Brigade relieved 173rd Brigade in the line and 41st Bn. of 11th Australian Brigade. Brigade Headquarters at C.25.b.5.2.	
C.25.b.5.2.	Sept. 2nd.		At 5.30 a.m. 229th Brigade attacked the enemy holding a line in front of MOISLAINS. Ultimate objective NURLU. Attack was not successful and we took up an advanced line West of MOISLAINS taking a few prisoners and guns. 12th Som.L.I. attacked on Right, 14th Rl.Highlrs. on Left and 16th Devons in Reserve.	
	Night 4/5th.		Took up a line along the Canal W. of MOISLAINS and were relieved by elements of 47th Division and 230th Brigade. Units returned to a bivouac area N. of CLERY Sur SOMME. (B.23.d. and B.30.a.)	
B.26.b.9.5.	5/6th.		Brigade remained in above bivouac area.	
AIZECOURT le HAUT.	6th		Brigade moved to a bivouac area in AIZECOURT le HAUT.	
TEMPLEUX la FOSSE.	7th.		Brigade moved to a bivouac area near LONGAVESNES, with Brigade Hd.Qrs. as in margin.	
LONGA- VESNES.	Night 8/9th.		229th Brigade relieved 231st Brigade in the line according to Brigade Order No.72 attached.	
	9th.		No action took place. B.G.C., R.HOARE wounded and evacuated. Lt.Col. SPENCE-JONES took over temporary command.	
	10th.		229th Brigade attacked the enemy positions and high ground W. of ROUSSOY, in accordance with Brigade Order No.73 attached. Attack met with small success and by 9 p.m. the same night we were back on our original line.	
TEMPLEUX la FOSSE.	Night 10/11th.		230th Brigade relieved 229th Brigade in the line, in accordance with Brigade Order No.74 attached. 229th Brigade less 12th Som.L.I. bivouacked near LONGAVESNES, 12th Som.L.I. bivouacked near TEMPLEUX la FOSSE.	
	11th.		14th Rl.Highlrs. and 16th Devons moved to area immediately W. of TEMPLEUX la FOSSE. Brigadier General F.S. THACKERAY (Highland Light Inf.) took command of the Brigade vice Brig./	

[Top margin, inverted handwriting:] HQ 229 Infy Bde 9/6
A number of signatures carried out by the 229 Brigade from September 2nd to 25th (4/18) 3 attacks

Army Form C. 2118.

WAR DIARY
or
INTELLIGENCE SUMMARY.

(Erase heading not required.)

Instructions regarding War Diaries and Intelligence Summaries are contained in F. S. Regs., Part II. and the Staff Manual respectively. Title pages will be prepared in manuscript.

Place	Date	Hour	Summary of Events and Information	Remarks and references to Appendices
	SEPTEMBER 1918.			
	11th contd.		Brig.Gen.R.HOARE to England (wounded).	
	12th to 15th.		No change of location. Reorganization within units took place and refitting.	
	Night 16/17th.		16th Devons under orders of 231st Brigade and 12th Som.L.I. under orders of 230th Brigade moved to a forward area.	
	17th.		16th Devons and 12th Som.L.I. came under direct orders of 231st and 230th Brigades respectively.	
	17/18th.		229th Bde.Hd.Qrs. moved to Battle Hd.Qrs. at FAUSTIN QUARRY. 14th Rl.Highlrs, 229th L.T.M. Battery and 'B' Coy. 74th M.G.Bn. moved to vicinity of FAUSTIN QUARRY in accordance with Brigade Orders Nos. 75 and 76 attached, in preparation for attack on Sept. 18th.	
K.5.d.1.1.	18th		Advance of 230th and 231st Brigades (with 12th Som.L.I. and 16th Devons attached, respectively) to 2nd objective was successful. 904 prisoners (all ranks) and a few guns were captured by the Division.	
	Night 19/20th.		16th Devons and 12th Som.L.I. came under orders of 229th Brigade.	
"	20/21st.		229th Brigade manned the Green Line (1st objective) in anticipation of attack on 21st. 14th Rl.Highlrs and 16th Devons in line and 12th Som.L.I. and 9th Londons (attached) in Brigade Support in TEMPLEUX QUARRIES.	
TEMPLEUX QUARRIES.	21st.		Brigade Hd.Qrs. moved to TEMPLEUX QUARRIES at 5.40 a.m. At an early hour reports indicated that the battle was developing favourably, as at 7.30 a.m. Division reported CAT POST captured by 231st Brigade and success signals by 230th Brigade on their objective. At 10 a.m. Black Watch were put at disposal of 230th Brigade. B.G.C., 230th Brigade called on this battalion by Priority wire at 11.40 a.m. via Division. Wire received at 12.25 p.m. and orders were immediately issued to Black Watch, who had been previously warned, to move to RED Line and they were replaced in GREEN Line by 12th Som.L.I. At 11.40 a.m. Division reported (wire received 12.45 p.m.) our troops in GILLEMONT FARM and enemy/	

Army Form C. 2118.

WAR DIARY
or
INTELLIGENCE SUMMARY.
(Erase heading not required.)

Instructions regarding War Diaries and Intelligence Summaries are contained in F. S. Regs., Part II. and the Staff Manual respectively. Title pages will be prepared in manuscript.

Place	Date	Hour	Summary of Events and Information	Remarks and references to Appendices
	SEPTEMBER 1918.			
	21st contd.		enemy in CAT POST. At 12.30 p.m. (wire received 1.40 p.m.) Division report made it apparent that the enemy had counter attacked heavily and the 230th Brigade had been driven out of QUENNEMONT FARM and was much reduced in numbers, and at 1.50 p.m. (wire received 2.37 p.m.) Division reported them in the RED Line. At 5.25 p.m. (wire received 9.07 p.m.) both Brigades were reported back on the RED Line.	
			In the meantime acting on orders received from Division at 1.50 p.m., 16th Devons were ordered to take up a position in the BELLICOURT Road and to come under orders of 231st Brigade on arrival. They were replaced in GREEN Line by 8th Londons. At 7.30 p.m. a verbal message was received from Division to the effect that the 1/12 L.N.Lancs (Pioneers) were moving to the old jumping off line and would come under orders of 229th Brigade.	
	Night 22/23rd.		229th Brigade (with 15th Suffolks attached) took over the front line in accordance with Brigade Order No.77 attached.	
	23rd.		American Advanced Parties arrived.	
	Night 23/24th.		Each battalion in line pushed out a post about 200 yds. E.of our line. These were wired and ordered to be held by day.	
	Night 24/25th.		229th Brigade relieved by 5 Coys. of 106th American Regiment, and bivouaced in vicinity of FAUSTINE QUARRY. (in accordance with Brigade Order No 78 attached.)	
Bde.Hd.Qrs. CORBIE.	25th.		229th Brigade Group (less Transport moving by road) entrained at TINCOURT and detrained at CORBIE and billeted in area CORBIE - LA NEUVILLE.	
Bde.Hd.Qrs. BOURCQ.	27th, 28th and 29th.		229th Brigade Group entrained at MERICOURT and detrained at MOURQUIT and were billeted in HAM en ARTOIS Area. Battalions as follows :-	
			Black Watch - BOURCQ.	
			16th Devons - HAM en ARTOIS.	
			12th Som.L.I. - MANQUEVILLE.	
			229th L.T.M.B. - BOURCQ.	

O.J.M. Tuck
Captain,
Brigade Major,
229th Infantry Brigade.

NARRATIVE OF OPERATIONS

Carried out by 229th Infantry Brigade, from 1st to 16th September 1918.

On the night of September 1st/2nd the 229th Brigade relieved the 173rd Brigade (58th Division) and the 41st Bn. of the 11th Australian Brigade in the line S.W. of BOUCHAVESNES, in preparation for the Fourth Army attack.

At 5.30 a.m. September 2nd, the Brigade attacked, in depth. The 12th Somerset Light Inf. leading, the 14th Royal Highlanders in Support, with orders to come into line on the Left of the Somersets as soon as MOISLAINS had been passed, and the 16th Devon Regt. in Brigade Reserve.
Difficulty had been found in reaching the Infantry Forming Up Line, on the greater part of the front of attack, as the enemy had pushed out a line of M.G. Posts during the night and was occupying BROUSSA Trench.
These elements of the enemy were inside the Barrage Start Line and had to be cleared before the Barrage could be properly followed, with the result that the advancing Infantry lost close touch with the Barrage from the start, and were unable to catch it up in the rough ground, intersected with old trenches and wire.
Soon after starting the right of the leading battalion, jumping off from SCUTARI Trench, came under a heavy enfilade fire on their right from HAUT ALLAINS. The battalion instinctively swung towards the opposition, cleared the village, and took about 70 prisoners, which with the exception of the wounded, and those immediately employed as Stretcher Bearers, were taken over by the Australians who had arrived upon the scene.
The 12th Som.L.I. then faced more Northwards towards its proper first objective, with the 14th Rl.Highlrs. on their Left.
Previous to crossing the Canal five enemy field guns had been met with and captured. (These guns were out of action due to the previous day's fighting).
On passing through C.24.a. and c. the battalion came under enfilade M.G. fire from MOISLAINS on their left, and at the same time a battery of enemy field guns in the open shelled them heavily from about D.13.b.8.4. Enemy Rifle and M.G. fire was also encountered from M.G's in D.19.central and D.25.central. Hand to hand fighting was experienced round the hutments in C.24.b. while the enfilade fire from MOISLAINS was continuous. Numerous casualties among the officers of the leading battalions were incurred, and under this harrassing fire they were not able to reach OPERA Trench on the left though the right of the Right battalion reached the outskirts of AIZECOURT le HAUT before being driven back.
At   a.m. the enemy counter attacked from the N.E. and E. in a most determined manner, but suffered heavily from the supporting fire of the M.G's of 'B' Coy., 74th M.G.Bn. who came promptly into action near the copse in C.22.d. and the leading enemy were cut down at close range, and the remainder quickly withdrew suffering casualties as they retired.
Our line then re-established itself in BROUSSA Trench and N. and S. of it, and had to put up with continual shelling with Gas and H.E. shells throughout the rest of the day.

Next day the line was advanced to MOISLAINS Trench and AUSPACH Trench. The Southern half of the village of MOISLAINS was then cleared by the 16th Devon Regt. and 14th Rl.Highlrs. while the 142nd Brigade 47th Division, cleared the Northern half.

The line was finally advanced at dusk on the 4th to the Canal bank at C.18.b.4.9. where touch was gained with the 47th Division, thence to the Slag Heap in C.24.central and C.30.central where touch was gained with the Australian Brigade on our Right.

On the/

On the night of the 4/5th September the 229th Brigade was relieved by two battalions of the 47th Division and the 230th Brigade, and bivouaced 1 mile N.of SUZY Sur SOMME.

On the 6th September the Brigade marched to AIZECOURT le HAUT and bivouaced for the night, moving to LONGAVESNES on the 7th, with Brigade Headquarters at TEMPLEUX la FOSSE. During this march the 229th Brigade was in Divisional Reserve, and was following up the successful advance of the 230th and 231st Brigades.

On the night of the 8/9th September the Brigade relieved the 231st Brigade in the line E.of VILLERS FAUCON and St.EMILIE, with the 16th Devon Regt. on the Right, the 14th Rl.Highlrs. on the Left and the 12th Som.L.I. in Brigade Reserve.

Brigadier General R.HOARE, D.S.O. was wounded near his Headquarters in LONGAVESNES on the 9th September and Lieut Colonel SPENCE JONES, D.S.O. 24th Welsh Regt. temporarily took command of the Brigade.

During the night of the 9/10th and morning of 10th September the Brigade carried out an attack on the high ground running from St.EMILE to RONNSOY thence S.W.to F.25.d. The greater part of this objective - i.e. as far as F.20.d. was taken by the 16th Devon Regt. and 14th Rl.Highlrs. but the retention of this ground was contingent on the capture of EPEHY by the 58th Division, who however could not make good their initial gains with the result that that, by 9 p.m. we had given up TEA POST, the last hold we had on the high ground and were back in our original line. Heavy casualties were suffered, and the Brigade was relieved that night by the 230th Brigade; Brigade Headquarters and 12th Som.L.I. moving to TEMPLEUX la FOSSE, and 16th Devon Regt. and 14th Rl. Highlanders to LONGAVESNES on relief, and on the 11th September the two last named battalions moved to the area immediately W.of TEMPLEUX la FOSSE.

The period from September 12th to 15th was spent in reorganizing and refitting in preparation for any further fighting that was to follow.

On September 15th Brigadier General F.S.THACKERAY, D.S.O.,M.C., Highland Light Infantry took over Command of the Brigade from Lieut Colonel SPENCE-JONES, D.S.O. 24th Welsh Regt. who had been temporarily Commanding the Brigade vice Brigadier General R.HOARE, D.S.O. wounded, to England.

On the night September 16/17th the 16th Devon Regt. and 12th Som. L.I. were moved to forward areas occupied by the 231st and 230th Brigades respectively.

NARRATIVE OF OPERATIONS

Carried out by 229th Infantry Brigade from 17th to 25th Sept.1918.

On the 17th September the 16th Bn.Devonshire Regt. and 12th Bn. Som.L.I. passed to the Command of B.G.C.,231st and 230th Infantry Brigades respectively. In the evening 229th Brigade Headquarters, 14th Bn.Royal Highlanders, 229th L.T.M.Battery and Headquarters 'B' Coy. 74th M.G.Bn. moved to Battle Headquarters at FAUSTINE QUARRY. At 5.20 a.m. on the 18th September the Division attacked, the Brigade consisting of the above units being in Divisional Reserve.

On the night of 19th/20th September the 16th Bn. Devon Regt. and 12th Bn.Som.L.I. came under Command of B.G.C. 229th Infantry Bde. and were located near FAUSTINE QUARRY. On the night of 20th/21st Sept. the 229th Infantry Brigade manned the GREEN Line (the 1st objective of the 18th instant) in anticipation of an attack on 21st by the 230th and 231st Infantry Brigades, the 14th Bn.Royal Highlanders being on the Right and the 16th Bn.Devonshire Regt. on the Left, the 12th Bn.Som. L.Inf. and the 8th London Regt. who were attached from the 174th Infantry Brigade, 58th Division, being in Reserve in the TEMPLEUX QUARRIES.

Early in the morning of 21st, Brigade Headquarters was moved to TEMPLEUX QUARRIES. At 10 a.m. the 14th Bn.Rl.Highlrs. were put at the disposal of 230th Infantry Brigade. B.G.C.,230th Brigade called on this battalion at 11.40 a.m. via Division, (wire received at 12.25 p.m. and orders were immediately issued to Royal Highlanders,who had previously been warned, to move to RED Line and they were replaced in GREEN Line by 12th Bn.Som.L.I.
At 1.50 p.m. orders were received for 16th Bn.Devon Regt. to take up position in BELLICOURT Road and to come under orders of B.G.C.,231st Infantry Brigade. They were replaced in GREEN Line by 8th London Regt. At 7.20 p.m. a verbal message was received from Division to the effect that 1/12th L.N.Lancs. (Pioneers) were moving to the original forming up line, and that they and a Coy. of the Life Guards M.G.Bn. who were already in position there, came under orders of B.G.C.,229th Infantry Brigade.

On the night of the 22nd/23rd B.G.C.,229th Infantry Brigade took over Command of front line from Right Divisional Boundary to CAT POST (exclusive)and 16th Devon Regt. and 14th Rl.Highlrs. reverted to, and 15th Suffolk Regt. came under his Command. 15th Suffolk Regt. on the Right and 14th Rl.Highlrs. next them on their Left remained in their former positions in the front line, but the Royal Highlrs. extended their Left to include BENJAMIN Post which was taken over from the 25th Royal Welsh Fusiliers. The 16th Devon Regt. moved forward from BELLICOURT Road and relieved the remainder of 25th Royal Welsh Fus. from BENJAMIN POST to CAT POST both exclusive, with one Company in BENJAMIN SWITCH. The 12th Som.L.I. moved into Support in ARTAXERXES Post and HUSSAR Road. A lot of Patrolling was done by each Battalion in the Line and touch was kept with the enemy.

On the morning of the 23rd, orders were received for the 230th Infantry Brigade on the Right and the 229th Infantry Brigade on the Left to make an attack at 2.30 a.m. on the 24th against the BLUE Line from QUENNEMONT Farm to STAVE Trench inclusive, this was cancelled about midday.
About 5 p.m. an Advance party of 106th American Regt. arrived and were sent out to Battalions.

On the night of the 23rd/24th Platoon Posts were pushed out about 200 to 250 yards by each battalion, dug in and wired, and ordered to be held by day and night.
Many patrols were sent out and touch was kept with the enemy by constant patrolling.
At about 10 p.m. five companies 106th American Regt. commenced to arrive and relieved the 229th Infantry Brigade.

The/

The 229th Infantry Brigade moved back to bivouac in the vicinity of FAUSTINE QUARRY.

During the time the 229th Infantry Brigade was holding the front line a lot of trouble was occasioned by the telephone lines to the front being continuously cut by shelling which was at times intense, but in spite of this by dint of very hard work on the part of the linesmen, communications were kept going practically continuously.

229th Infantry Brigade.

Casualties incurred during Operations September 2nd to September 25th.

Date.	Bde. Hd.Qrs.				16th Devons.				12th Som.L.I.				14th Rl.Highlrs.				229th L.T.M.Bty.			
	Killed.		Wounded.		Killed.		Wounded.		Killed.		Wounded.		Killed.		Wounded.		Killed.		Wounded.	
	Off.	O.R.	Off.	O.R.	Off.	O.R.	Off.	O.R.	Off.	O.R.	Off.	O.R.	Off.	O.R.	Off.	O.R.	Off.	O.R.	Off.	O.R.
Sept. 2nd to 9th.	-	-	1	-	1	26	4	134	5	38	6	159	3	33	13	156	-	-	-	1
Sept. 10th to 17th.	-	-	-	-	-	13	2	27	-	1	4	114	-	4	2	23	-	-	-	-
Sept. 18th to 25th.	1	-	-	-	1	11	6	60	1	4	2	59	-	11	3	57	-	-	-	3
Total.	1	-	1	-	2	50	12	221	6	43	12	332	3	48	18	236	-	-	-	4

	Killed.		Wounded.	
	Off.	O.R.	Off.	O.R.
Total Casualties for Phase Sept. 2nd to Sept. 9th	9	97	24	450
" " " " 10th to " 17th	-	18	8	164
" " " " 18th to " 25th	4	25	11	179
Total	13	140	43	793.

229 Brigade Order no 70   Copy No.

1. The Brigade will reorganise on the line
   ANGORA trench C.16
   BROUSSA trench C.22
   SCUTARI trench C.28a
   and hold that line.

2. The 229 Brigade will hold the left portion of the line.
   12 Somerset L.I.   on the right
   14 Royal Highders   in the centre
   16 Devons   on the left
   Machine guns to be distributed, and arranged in depth on a defensive scheme.

3. Every effort must be made to gain and maintain touch with Brigades on the Right and Left.

4. An S.O.S line is being arranged.

5. All men in front of the line stated in para 1 will be withdrawn forthwith or as truck Issued at.

Copies:
O.C. 16 Divns   H.Q. 142 Bde.
   12 Somerset   " 7 Aust "
   14 R.H.   O.P. 229 T.M.B.
H.Q 230 Bde   " A Co 74 M.G Bn
  " 231 "   " B Co " " "
  " 74th Divn.

2-9-18

Sy Tudor
Captn
Brigade Major
229 Inf Bde

P.T.O

Bde Order No 70.

1. The Brigades will reorganise on the line
   ANGORA trench C.16.
   BROUSSA trench C.22
   SCUTARI trench C.28.a
   and hold that line.

2. The 229 Brigade will hold the left portion of the line.
   12 Somerset L.I. on the right
   14 Royal Highdrs in the Centre
   16 Devons on the left
   Machine guns to be distributed and arranged in depth on a defensive scheme

3. Every effort must be made to gain and maintain touch with Brigades on the Right & Left.

4. An S.O.S. line is being arranged. All men in rear of this line will be withdrawn.

5. All men in front of the line stated in para 1 will be withdrawn forthwith, or at dusk

Units will report dispositions as soon as reorganisation is complete

Capt.
Brigade Major
229 Inf Bde

229th. Brigade Order No.70.

1. The Brigade will reorganise on the Line;-

   ANGORA   trench C16.
   BROUSSA trench C22.
   SCUTARI trench C28a.
   and hold that line.

2. The 229 Brigade will hold the left portion of the line.
   12th. Somerset L.I.   on the right.
   14th. Rl.Hdrs.   in the centre.
   16th. Devons.   on the left.
   machine guns to be distributed and arranged in depth on a defensive scheme.

3. Every effort must be made to gain and maintain touch with Brigades on the right and left.

4. An S.O.S. line is being arranged.

5. All men in front of the line stated in para 1 will be withdrawn forthwith.

3-9-18.

Captain,
Brigade Major,
229th. Infantry Brigade.

229th. Brigade Order No.70.
----

1. The Brigade will reorganise on the Line;-

   ANGORA   trench C16.
   BROUSSA   trench C22.
   SCUTARI   trench C28a.
   and hold that line.

2. The 229 Brigade will hold the left portion of the line.
   12th.Somerset L.I.   on the right.
   14th.Rl.Hdrs.   in the centre.
   16th.Devons.   on the left.
   machine guns to be distributed and arranged in depth on a defensive scheme.

3. Every effort must be made to gain and maintain touch with Brigades on the right and left.

4. An S.O.S.line is being arranged.

5. All men in front of the line stated in para 1 will be withdrawn forthwith.

                                                  Captain,
                                         Brigade Major,
3-9-18.   229th. Infantry Brigade.

229 Inf Bde Order No 1.

1. 229 Inf Brigade will be relieved in the line tonight 4th/5th Septr.

2. The 19th London Regt of 141st Brigade will relieve the 16th Devons and 14th R.H. and the 10th Buffs and 15th Suffolks of 230th Brigade will relieve the 12th Somerset L.I.

   Details as to guides etc to be arranged between Commanding Officers concerned.

3. On relief, 229 Brigade will come into Divisional Reserve and be bivouaced in B.23.d approx.

   Brigade H.Q. at B.26.c.9.0 will open on completion of relief.

   Guides to new area are being shown bivouac locations by Staff Captain.

4. 229 L.T.M.B will be withdrawn from the line on receipt of this order.

5. Completion of relief to be wired Priority to this H.Q.

Copies to
16th Devon   1st Aust Bde
12 Somerset   229 T.M.B
14 R H   230 Inf Bde
142 Inf Bde   231 Inf Bde
141 Inf Bde
G.4 Divn   4-9-18

A/M Tuck
Captn
Brigade Major
229 Inf Bde

SECRET

229th BRIGADE ORDER No. 72.

Copy No. 15

Sept. 8th 1918.

1. 229th Brigade Group will relieve the 231st Brigade Group in the line tonight 8/9th September, as follows :-

    (a) 16th Devons to relieve 24th Welsh from L.1.c.4.7. to F.25.b.2.7.
    (b) 1 Coy. 12th Som.L.I. to relieve a portion of 24th Welsh and 10th K.S.L.I. from F.25.b.2.7. to F.19.d.2.5.
    (c) 14th Rl.Highlrs. will take over the remainder of the line to Northern Divisional Boundary at F.14.a.2.9. The Company of 12th Som.L.I. will come under orders of O.C., 14th Rl.Highlrs.
    (d) The 12th Som.L.I. (less 1 Coy) and 229th L.T.M.Battery will be in Reserve in E.30.a.

2. (a) O.C., 'B' Coy. 74th M.G.Bn. will attach 1 section to 16th Devons and 1 Section to 14th Rl.Highlrs. The remainder of the Company will relieve Reserve portion of 'A' Coy. and move forward to E.30.a.
    (b) The 2nd Life Guards M.G.Coy. will move to F.23.c.8.3.

3. Headquarters at present are as follows :-
    24th Welsh   -   E.29.d.7.3.
    10th K.S.L.I.   -   E.29.d.1.8. (SPUR QUARRY)
    25th R.W.F.   -   F.23.d.2.7.

4. (a) 24th Welsh will be established in vicinity of FAUSTINE QUARRY (K.5.c.8.1.) with Patrols pushed forward to gain touch with the right of the Devons and the approaches from the South, and be prepared to form a Defensive Flank.
    (b) The Left of the Australian Brigade is near Cross Roads in K.12.d.3.4.

5. O.C., 14th Rl.Highlrs. will exercise greatest care in taking over the line up to the Northern Divisional Boundary.

6. Relief complete will be reported by the quickest possible method to this Headquarters. Code Word will be "BRAMBLE".

7. Details not mentioned in this order will be arranged between Commanding Officers concerned.

8. Boundary between Battalions will be a straight line from F.19.d.2.5. to F.21.a.0.0. thence due E. through F.21.central, F.24.central.

9. An Advanced Report Centre will be established at E.29.d.1.8. (SPUR QUARRY).

10. Brigade Battle Headquarters will be at K.3.d.2.8.

11. ACKNOWLEDGE.

Issued at 9.45pm

Captain,
Brigade Major,
229th Infantry Brigade.

Copies to :-
No.1	B.G.C., 229th Inf.Bde.	9	'B' Coy. 74th M.G.Bn.
2	16th Devon Regt.	10	O.C.Sect.439th Fld.Coy.R.E.
3	12th Som.L.I.	11	175th Infantry Brigade
4	14th Rl.Highlrs.	12	Right Flank Aust. Bde.
5	229th L.T.M.Battery	13	Bde.Sig.Officer
6	74th (Yeo) Division.	14	Staff Captain,
7	231st Infantry Brigade	15	War Diary
8	'B' Coy. 2nd Life Guards M.G.Bn.	16	File.
		17	24th Welsh
		18	44th Brigade R.F.A.

SECRET

229th BRIGADE ORDER No. 73.

Copy No. 21

9 Sep/18

1. 56th Division is attacking PEIZIERE and EPEHY, and Railway Line in F.7.b.& c. with a second objective for Right Bn - trenches in F.8.a.& d. and F.2.c. - at 5.15 a.m. tomorrow under creeping barrage.

2. 6th London Regt. of 173rd Infantry Brigade prior to Zero is pushing forward a line of Posts through line F.7.b. and F.1.d.

3. The 229th Infantry Brigade will advance the line as follows with three distinct moves :-

    (a) Immediately on receipt of this order 16th Devons and 14th Rl.Highlrs. will make good the spurs in F.26.a. - F.20.central and F.19.b.
        i. 1 Coy. 16th Devons will secure their Right flank in trench elements at F.25.d.4.2.
        ii. 2 Coys. 16th Devons will establish themselves on high ground in trenches in vicinity of TEA Post (F.26.a.) and consolidate.
        iii. 1 Coy. 16th Devons will remain in Reserve at F.25.central.
        iv. 2 Coys. 14th Rl.Highlrs. will make good trenches in F.20.a.& c.

    (b) To take place at Zero Hour.
        1 Coy. 14th Rl.Highlrs. in conformity with 6th London Regt. on their Left will relinquish their defensive flank in E.18.a.& b. bringing it forward to trenches in F.13.a.

    (c) Exact time cannot be fixed, but will depend upon success at EPEHY and will not take place before 6.0 5 a.m.
        i. 2 Coys. 14th Rl.Highlrs. shewn under para. (a.iv.) above will advance to trench line F.20.d.3.0. to F.20.b.9.5.
        ii. 1 Coy. 14th Rl.Highlrs. from F.20.b.9.5. to F.14.d.3.2.
        iii. 1 Coy. 14th Rl.Highlrs. (shewn in para b. above) will advance and occupy trench line in F.14.d.3.5. to Cross Roads N.of F.14.central.
        iv. 1 Coy. 14th Rl.Highlrs. in Reserve in trenches in F.13.d. (Note :- 5 Coys. of 14th Rl.Highlrs. include attd. Coy. from 12th Som.L.I.)

4. (a) O.C.,16th Devons will not lose touch with Australians on Right and will hold trench in L.1.a.
   (b) O.C.,14th Rl.Highlrs. will be responsible for establishing a Liaison Post at KNOLL POST in F.8.d.6.1. on objective being gained by 6th London Regt.

5. Bombardment to cover this advance will be provided by four Brigades of Field Artillery, with Heavy Artillery co-operating.

6. Advanced Report Centre will be established at Headquarters, 16th Devons in SPUR QUARRY (E.29.d.1.8.) where all messages will be sent.

7. 12th Som.L.I. will not move until order is received from Brigade Headquarters, and will provide a runner at SPUR QUARRY.

8. On reaching final objective active patrolling will be carried out, and success will be exploited in the direction of RONSSEY and BASSEE BOULOGNE.

9. Zero Hour for this Brigade will be 5.15 a.m.

10. ACKNOWLEDGE.

[signature] Tuck

Issued at ....10 p.m....

Captain,
Brigade Major,
229th Infantry Brigade,

Copies to :-

```
No. 1   O.C., 229th Infantry Brigade
    2   16th Devon Regt.
    3   12th Som.L.I.
    4   14th Rl.Highlrs.
    5   229th L.T.M.Battery
    6   'B' Coy. 74th M.G.Bn.
    7   'B' Coy. 2nd Life Guards M.G.Bn.
    8   173rd Infantry Brigade
    9   174th Infantry Brigade
   10   10th Australian Brigade
   11   231st Infantry Brigade
   12   74th (Yeo) Division
   13   44th Brigade R.F.A.
   14   Lt.Col. KINNEAR, D.S.O.
   15           do
   16   Staff Captain
   17   Bde.Sig.Officer
   18   'B' Squad. Northumberland Hussars
   19   No.1 Sect. 439th Fld.Coy.R.E.
   20   182nd Tunnelling Coy.
   21   War Diary
   22   File.
```

SECRET.   Copy No. 18

229th BRIGADE ORDER No.74.

Sept. 10th 1918.

1. The 229th Brigade Group will be relieved by the 230th Brigade Group in the line tonight 10/11th instant, and move into Divisional Reserve.

2. O.C., Right and Left Battalions will reorganize their line with three companies in line and 1 in support. Boundaries remain unchanged.
   To give effect to this O.C., 14th Rl.Highlrs. must arrange the six companies now under his command so that they may readily be relieved by three companies of the incoming unit. He will also gain touch on his left flank, and great care will be exercised in handing over the liaison post.

3. Units will relieve each other as under :-

16th Devons	16th Sussex
14th Rl.Highlrs.	10th Buffs
12th Som.L.I.	15th Suffolks.
229th L.T.M.Battery	230th L.T.M.Battery
'B' Coy. 74th M.G.Bn.)	By 2 Coys. to be detailed
'B' Coy. 2nd Life Guards M.G.Bn.)	by 74th M.G.Bn.

4. All details not mentioned in this order will be arranged between Commanding Officers concerned.

5. The Staff Captain will shew representatives of units (taken from transport lines) the location of bivouac area.

6. 1 Sect. Tunnelling Coy, 'B' Squad. Northumberland Hussars, will come under orders of B.G.C., 230th Brigade on completion of relief.

7. Brigade Headquarters will close on completion of relief and open at the same time at J.4.b.4.9.

8. Relief complete will be wired to this Headquarters. Code Word will be "FOX".

9. ACKNOWLEDGE.

                                            Captain,
                                            Brigade Major,
                                            229th Infantry Brigade.

Issued at 3pm

Copies to :-

        No.1 B.G.C., 229th Infantry Brigade,
           2 16th Devon Regt.
           3 12th Som.L.I.
           4 14th Rl.Highlrs.
           5 229th L.T.M.Battery
           6 'B' Coy. 74th M.G.Bn.
           7 'B' Coy. 2nd Life Guards M.G.Bn.
           8 173rd Infantry Brigade,
           9 10th Australian Brigade
          10 230th Infantry Brigade,
          11 74th (Yeo) Division,
          12 44th Brigade R.F.A.
          13 Staff Captain,
          14 Bde.Sig.Officer,
          15 'B' Squad. Northumberland Hussars
          16 No.1 Sect. 439th Fld.Coy.R.E.
          17 182nd Tunnelling Coy.
          18 War Diary,
          19 File.

SECRET   Copy No. 9

BRIGADE ORDER No. 75.

                                                                 16th Sept. 1918.

1.   The IIIrd Corps is continuing the attack in conjunction with Corps
and Armies on either flank, with a view to securing a position affording
good observation of the HINDENBURG Line.
     The 1st Australian Division will be on our right and the 18th Division
will be on our left.
     Z day and zero hour will be notified later.

2.   There will be three objectives.

          First Objective .... GREEN LINE
          Second Objective .... RED LINE
          LINE OF EXPLOITATION .... BLUE LINE.

     The objectives and Divisional and Brigade Boundaries are shown on the
attached map. TOINE POST will be inclusive to Right Brigade on 1st Objective
and BENJAMIN POST inclusive to Left Brigade on 2nd Objective. The map also
shows the dugouts previously existing in the area to be attacked.

3.   The 38th Division, with 96th, 95th and 94th Inf.Regts. from right to
left, is believed to be holding the enemy line from TEMPLEUX le GUERARD
to RONSSOY.

4.   Distribution of Troops.

     230th Brigade will be the right attacking Brigade, 231st Brigade will be
the left attacking Brigade. To each Brigade one battalion of 229th Brigade
will be attached, 16th Devon Regt. to 231st Brigade, 12th Somerset L.I. to
230th Brigade. These battalions will come under the orders of the attacking
Brigades on Y day.
     To each attacking Brigade will also be attached :-
½ Troop Northumberland Hussars for intercommunication.
1 Section R.E.
1 Machine Gun Coy. (less 2 Sections)
Detachment Tunnelling Coy. with knowledge of the forward area.
     Assembly area allotted to attacking Brigades is East of a North and
South line through E.28.central.
     230th and 231st Brigades will take over their attacking fronts on X/Y
night.
     229th Brigade (less 2 Battns.)to which one M.G.Company will be attached
and 229th L.T.M.Battery will be in Divisional Reserve. It will be located
about FAUSTINE Quarry in K.5.c.on Y/Z night.
     Units will reconnoitre forthwith for assembling positions in vicinity
of FAUSTINE QUARRY. 14th Rl.Highlrs. will reconnoitre line of advance to
line occupied by 230th and 231st Brigades on Y/Z night.

5.   Method of Attack.

     Both Brigades will attack the 1st Objective with 2 Battns. and will
"leap frog" two Battalions through for the attack upon the 2nd Objective.
     230th Brigade will on Y/Z night, move its right battalion South of
the COLOGNE River and will be allotted ground by the 1st Australian Division
as far South as L.8.a.0.0. 230th Brigade will attack TEMPLEUX le GUERARD
and the Quarries East of it with the battalion South of the COLOGNE River
moving in a N.E.direction in close co-operation with the left of the 1st
Australian Division which will attack BOLSOVER SWITCH in L.4.c. simultaneous
with the 230th Brigade attack upon the Quarries in L.3.a.and b. The Left
battalion, 230th Brigade will attack TEMPLEUX and the QUARRIES from the N.W.
Special parties will be detailed for the mopping up of TEMPLEUX le GUERARD
and the QUARRIES.
     The general line of advance of the 231st Brigade will be in an E.N.E.
direction along the spur in F.26.a. and b. - F.20.d. thence in an Easterly
direction to the 1st Objective.
     The advance of both Brigades from the 1st to the 2nd Objectives will be
along the high ground in a E.N.E.direction, 230th Brigade keeping touch with
1st Australian Brigade on the Divisional Boundary.

                                                       Objectives/

Objectives gained will be consolidated and the defence organised in depth. In view of the probability of the enemy having registered the existing trench system, troops should, when possible, dig in on lines some 300 yards in advance of the old systems.

Special mopping up parties will be detailed sufficiently large for the objectives captured to be thoroughly searched. Special attention is to be paid to the routes to be followed by troops passing through to take the second Objective, so as to avoid these troops getting delayed by uncompleted mopping up of localities.

Each Platoon will fire a GREEN Very Light on reaching the GREEN Line and a RED Very Light on reaching the RED Line. Special watch will be kept by F.O.O's for these "success" signals and they will be immediately reported.

The barrage will come down at zero on the North and South grid line between F.19. and F.20. The infantry forming up line will be 200 yards West of this line and will be taped prior to zero.

The infantry forming up line of the 1st Australian Division runs from the Divisional Boundary at L.1.d.7.0. thence through about L.4.d.0.0.

6. Line of Exploitation.

When the RED Line has been taken and consolidation is proceeding, every effort will be made to establish Posts in the BLUE Line, and especially to secure MALAKOFF Wood spur and QUENNEMONT FARM.

Certain batteries will move forward so soon as the RED Line has been secured, and will be prepared to cover posts established in the BLUE Line; the S.O.S. barrage for the Divisional front will be arranged to cover that line. (

7. Signal Communication.

(a) Brigade Forward Stations will be established for 230th Brigade about the Quarries East of TEMPLEUX le GUERARD, for 231st Brigade about CLIFF POST in F.20.d. Personnel for these Forward Stations will be provided in accordance with S.S.191. Divisional Signal Company will take over lines up to the Forward Stations as soon as Brigade H.Q. is established there.

(b) Visual.

A central Visual Station will be established in K.3.central. It will be connected by wire with Divisional H.Q. This visual station will be for the use of all formations. The Call will be V.S.

(c) Power Buzzers.

Each attacking Brigade will be provided with two complete loopsets. This will provide communication for 2 battalion H.Q., one Report Centre and one Brigade H.Q. Messages can be sent in clear when fighting is in progress at the discretion of C.O's.

(d) Wireless.

Wireless sets will be established at Brigade H.Q. and should move forward when Brigade H.Q. moves to the Forward Station.

(e) Pigeons.

Pigeons will be provided for use of Brigade and Battalion H.Q.

8. Royal Engineers.

The Field Coys. R.E.(less 2 Sections) and Pioneer Battn. will be under the orders of the C.R.E.

The C.R.E. will arrange for :-
(a) parties to assist the R.A. to clear wire and prepare crossings over trenches.
(b) special parties to reconnoitre for and develop water.
(c) improvement of forward roads in the Divisional area.

A forward R.E. dump is being formed from which Infantry Brigades can obtain material for consolidation. The C.R.E. will notify Infantry Brigades of the contents of the dump and its location.

9. Liaison.

Liaison will be made by special patrols under an officer with flank Divisions at the following places :-

(a) by 230th Bde./

- 3 -

(a) by 230th Brigade.
in BOLSOVER Switch about L.3.d.9.8.
on the RONSSOY - HARGICOURT Road L.4.b.4.5.
MALAKOFF Farm in F.30.
A.26.d.5.0.

(b) by 231st Brigade.
at Wood F.22.d.0.8.
in CAT POST F.24.a.2.9.
at A.14.c.1.0.

10. Secrecy.

The necessity for secrecy is to be impressed on all concerned. Reconnaissances should be reduced to a minimum. Listening sets are probably already installed in the HINDENBURG Line and no reference on the telephone East of Divisional H.Q. must be made to moves or to the operations.

11. Captured Guns.

In the event of the capture of hostile guns, information should be sent to the nearest Inf.Bde.H.Q. for transmission to the artillery, giving exact location of guns, nature of gun and whether ammunition is at hand. This information should be passed on to the C.R.A., who will arrange to send up personnel to man the guns. Spare parts, sights, etc. must not be removed as souvenirs from captured guns.

12. Roads.

Roads are allotted to this Division as under :-

VILLERS FAUCON - TEMPLEUX - RONSSOY.
VILLERS FAUCON - St. EMILIE - RONSSOY - F.30.a.
(to be used by 18th Division if required)

13. Aeroplanes.

(a) A contact aeroplane will fly over the Corps Front at :-

Zero 2 hours and 15 minutes.
Zero 5 hours.
Zero 7 hours.
and subsequently as ordered.

Troops will be specially warned to be on the look-out for these planes and to indicate their position by means of flares, rifles in rows and waving of helmets. Red flares only will be used.

Brigade and battalion H.Q. will display their ground signal sheets and strips when our aeroplanes are flying over the Divisional Front.

(a) Aeroplanes are being supplied to machine gun and bomb hostile batteries and columns of troops and transport on roads in rear of the BLUE Line.

(c) A counter-attack plane will be up continuously from daylight onwards with the sole mission of detecting the approach of enemy counter-attacks. The aeroplane will fly in the direction of the enemy dropping a WHITE Parachute flare as near to the counter-attacking troops as possible.

14. S.O.S.SIGNAL.

The IIIrd Corps and Australian Corps S.O.S.Signal is :-

RED over RED over RED.

15. TIME.

An Officer will visit Inf.Bde.H.Q. about 1 p.m. and 6-30 p.m. on Y day to synchronize watches. Synchronization must not be carried out by telephone East of Divisional H.Q.

and Bn HQ soonafter

16/

16. **HEADQUARTERS.**

    74th Div. H.Q.   in its present position.
    230th Bde.H.Q.   SPUR QUARRY (E.29.d.)
    231st Bde.H.Q.   E.23.b.7.2.
    229th Bde.H.Q.   FAUSTINE QUARRY (K.5.c.)

17. **ACKNOWLEDGE.**

                                                        A/M Tuck
                                                        Captain,
Issued at ..7.am.....   Brigade Major,
                                             229th Infantry Brigade.

    Copies to :- No. 1 B.G.C., 229th Inf.Bde.
                 X 2 14th Rl.Highlrs.
                 X 3 'B' Coy. 74th M.G.Bn.
                 X 4 229th L.T.M.Battery
                   5 1 Section 439th Fld.Coy.R.E.
                   6 Staff Captain
                   7 Brigade Signal Officer,
                   8 Brigade Intelligence Officer,
                   9 War Diary
                 10 File.

Maps issued only to recipients marked X.

WD

SECRET

Copy No. 9

Map Ref. 62c.1.N.E.
Scale 1:40,000.

229th BRIGADE ORDER No. 76.

September 17th 1918.

1. In accordance with Brigade Order No.75, 16th Devons and 12th Som.L.I. come under orders of B.G.C's 231st and 230th Infantry Brigades respectively on 17th instant.

2. Z day will be September 18th.
   The hour of ZERO will be notified by 3 p.m. on 17th instant.

3. (a) 14th Rl.Highlrs., 229th L.T.M.Battery and 1 Section 439th Fld.Coy. R.E. will move to the vicinity of FAUSTINE QUARRY on night of 17/18th instant. Move to be complete by 10 p.m.
   'B' Coy. 74th M.G.Bn. will remain in their present bivouac area.

   (b) Representatives of above Units, less 'B' Coy. 74th M.G.Bn. will meet the Staff Captain at 4.30 p.m. on 17th instant at K.5.c.6.1. who will shew them exact locations of assembly positions already reconnoitred.

4. Brigade Headquarters will close at 10 p.m. 17th instant and open at the same hour at FAUSTINE QUARRY (K.11.b.3.7.)

5. ACKNOWLEDGE.

Captain,
Brigade Major,
229th Infantry Brigade.

Issued at ...7am...

Copies to :-

No. 1 B.G.C., 229th Inf.Bde.
2 14th Rl.Highlrs.
3 229th L.T.M.Battery.
4 'B' Coy. 74th M.G.Bn.
5 1 Section, 439th Fld.Coy.R.E.
6 Staff Captain,
7 Brigade Signal Officer
8 "   Intelligence Officer
9 War Diary
10 File.

ADMINISTRATIVE INSTRUCTIONS

issued with Brigade Order No. 76.

Sept. 17th 1918.

1. **Supplies** will be drawn as follows :-

    (a) For consumption 18th - 7.30 a.m. on 17th from present dump.

    (b) For consumption 19th - 3 p.m. on 17th from Decauville Siding D.26.c.2.5.
    Supply wagons will be ret-urned to Train after delivery of rations for consumption 19th instant.

2. **Water.**

    (a) Drinking - from LONGAVESNES or TEMPLEUX LA FOSSE.

    (b) Animals - on 18th inst. TEMPLEUX LA FOSSE beside Drinking Water point.
    on 19th inst. same as on 18th or from K.10.c. if transport lines have moved forward by that time.

3. **Equipment.** Units will be equipped on the scale laid down in Table A of 74th Division Administrative Instructions dated 16-9-18 already issued.
Packs and not haversacks will be carried. Greatcoats, haversacks, blankets, spare underclothing &c will be dumped at transport lines on 17th instant.

4. **Transport.** Lines will be moved on 17th instant to vicinity of K.1.a.& b. where they will remain till the situation permits of further advance.
Baggage wagons will report to 14th Rl.Highlrs at 10 a.m. on 17th and remain with them till further orders.

5. **Ammunition** as follows will be carried :-

    (a) On the man - as in Table A of 74th Division Administrative Instructions dated 16-9-18.
    (b) On transport - complete echelons of S.A.A. plus 2 boxes Very Lights 1" D.1.White, 2 boxes S.O.S.Grenades and 1 box Message Carrying Rockets.
    (c) 229th L.T.M.Battery will draw 160 rounds Stokes ammunition from D.A.C.on 17th and take it to new area.

6. Units will reconnoitre the positions of the two forward dumps at F.25.a.4.7. and F.25.a.2.9. in case they hay have to draw from either of these later on.

6. **Medical** - Arrangements have been sent direct to all R.M.O's concerned.

7. **Provost Arrangements** have already been issued to all units.

Captain,
Staff Captain,
229th Infantry Brigade.

Copies to :-
14th Rl.Highlrs.
229th L.T.M.Battery,
'B' Coy. 74th M.G.Bn.
1 Section 439th Fld.Coy.R.E.

229th Brigade Order No. 77.   Copy No.

SECRET

para 1 (a) The 229 Brigade to which 15th SUFFOLKS will be attached will take over the RED LINE as far north as CAT POST exclusive

(b) North of this point the line will be held by 231st Brigade

(c) The 230th Brigade (less 15th Suffolks) will take over GREEN line from Southern Divisional Boundary to TOINE POST (exclusive).

(d) 8th London Regt. and responsibility for GREEN LINE north of TOINE POST (inclusive) will pass to 18th Division at 8 p.m. to-night

(e) 16th Devons & 14th R.H. will rejoin 229th Brigade on receipt of this order.

para 2.   229 Brigade will be disposed as follows:-

(a) 15th Suffolks will stand fast in RED LINE. H.Q. at F.28.d.7.9.

(b) 14th R.H. will hold RED LINE from F.30.a.1.0. inclusive to BENJAMIN POST inclusive

with three Companies in line
and one Company in Eastern
portion of ARTAXERXES POST.
H.Q. in ~~NEW QUERY~~ in F.29.b.0.15
(c) 16th Devons will hold RED LINE
from BENJAMIN POST exclusive
to CAT POST exclusive with three
companies in line and one
company in Reserve in SWITCH
TRENCH in F.23.C. H.Q. at
F.29.b.o.5.
(d) 12th Som. L.I. will be in
Brigade Reserve with three
Companies in HUSSAR ROAD in
F.23.c. and F.29 a. and b and d
and one company in Western
portion of ARTAXERXES POST.
H.Q. as ~~F.29.b.o.5.~~ at present

para 3.   Details not mentioned in
this order will be arranged
with Commanding Officers at
present in Line.

para 4 (a) In case of urgent necessity
14th R.H. may call on one
Company 12th Som L.I in
ARTAXERXES POST
(b) O.C. 12th Som L.I. in case of

enemy attack will act on his own initiative and not wait for orders from B.H.Q. and must therefore reconnoitre the Line to his Front.

para 5. Northern Divisional Boundary will now be F.19.c.0.4. CNIFFE POST inclusive – TOINE POST (exclusive) MILL LANE (inclusive) thence due EAST.

para 6. Completion of moves described above will be reported by wire and runner immediately, using surname of Commanding Officer as CODE WORD.

para 7. Acknowledge by wire.

J.M. Tuck
Captain,
Brigade Major,
229th Infantry Brigade.

22.9.18
Issued at 5.50pm

Copies to

O.C.	16th	Devons
"	12th	Som L I
"	14th	R.H.
"	8th	London Regt
"	15th	Suffolks
H.Q.	230th	Inf. Brigade
"	231st	" "
"	74th	(Yeo) Division
O.C.	B Coy	M G B
"	229th	L T M B
B.G.C.	229th	Inf Brigade

HEADQUARTERS
229th INFANTRY BDE
Date 20-9-18
No. 38

O.C.
16th Dwons
12th Somerset L.I.
14th R.H.
229 T.M.B.
"B" Coy 74th M.G. Bn

Ref warning order of to-day.
Reconnaissances will be
carried out forthwith.

A. Van Tuyl
Captn.
Brigade Major
229 Inf Bde

20-9-18

SECRET. WD

229th BRIGADE ORDER No. 77.

Copy No......

22nd September 1918.

1. (a) The 229th Brigade to which 15th Suffolks will be attached will take over the RED LINE as far North as CAT POST exclusive.
    (b) North of this point the line will be held by 231st Brigade.
    (c) 230th Brigade (less 15th Suffolks) will take over GREEN LINE from Southern Divisional Boundary to TOINE POST (exclusive).
    (d) 8th London Regt. and responsibility for GREEN LINE North of TOINE POST (inclusive) will pass to 18th Division at 8 p.m. tonight.
    (e) 16th Devons and 14th Rl.Highlrs. will rejoin 229th Brigade on receipt of this order.

2. 229th Brigade will be disposed as follows :-

    (a) 15th Suffolks will stand fast in RED LINE. H.Q. at F.28.d.7.9.
    (b) 14th Rl.Highlrs. will hold RED LINE from F.30.a.1.0. inclusive to BENJAMIN POST inclusive with 3 companies in line, and 1 coy. in Eastern portion of ARTAXERXES POST, H.Q. in NEW QUARRY in F.29.c.
    (c) 16th Devons will hold RED LINE from BENJAMIN POST exclusive to CAT POST exclusive with 3 Companies in Line and 1 Company in Reserve in SWITCH TRENCH in F.23.c. H.Q. at F.29.b.0.5.
    (d) 12th Som.L.I. will be in Brigade Reserve with 3 companies in HUSSAR ROAD in F.23.c. and F.29.a. and b. and 1 Coy. in Western portion of ARTAXERXES POST. H.Q. at F.29.b.0.5.

3. Details not mentioned in this order will be arranged with Commanding Officers at present in line.

4. (a) In case of urgent necessity 14th Rl.Highlrs. may call on 1 Coy. 12th Som.L.L. in ARTAXERXES POST.
    (b) O.C.,12th Som.L.I. in case of enemy attack will act on his own initiative and not wait for orders from Brigade Hd.Qrs. and must therefore reconnoitre the line to his front.

5. Northern Divisional Boundary will now be F.19.c.0.4. CLIFFE POST inclusive - TOINE POST (exclusive) MILL LANE (inclusive) thence due EAST.

6. Completion of moves described above will be reported by <u>wire</u> <u>and runner immediately</u> using surname of Commanding Officer as <u>CODE WORD</u>.

7. ACKNOWLEDGE by wire.

Issued at ....

Captain,
Brigade Major,
229th Infantry Brigade.

Copies to :-
    No.1 16th Devon Regt.
      2 12th Som.L.I.
      3 14th Rl.Highlrs.
      4 8th London Regt.
      5 15th Suffolk Regt.
      6 H.Q.,230th Inf.Bde.
    No.7 H.Q.,231st Infantry Bde.
      8 H.Q.,74th (Yeo) Division
      9 'B' Coy. 74th M.G.Bn.
     10 229th L.T.M.Battery
     11 B.G.C.,229th Inf.Bde.
     12 War Diary
     13 File.

SECRET WD

229th BRIGADE ORDER No.78

Copy No......
24th September 1918.

1. The 229th Brigade with 15th.Suffolks will be relieved by the 1st Battn. 106th American Regt. and E.Coy. 2nd Bn. 106th American Regt. tonight 24th/25th instant according to Table attached.

2. The following will be left in the line until the night Sept. 25/26th

    a. 2 officers per Battalion
    b. 2 N.C.O's per Company.

3. On relief Units of 229th Brigade will proceed to vicinity of FAUSTINE QUARRY.
A representative of each Unit will report one hour in advance to the Staff Captain in FAUSTINE QUARRY at K.11.b.3.7. where guides will be ready to guide units to bivouac area.
15th Suffolks after relief will move under orders issued by 230th Brigade.

4. Orders for move of transport are being issued direct to Battn. Transport Lines and Units in rear concerned.

5. Dismounted personnel of the Brigade will move by tactical trains to CORBIE Area on 25th Sept. The first train will probably leave TINCOURT about 10 a.m.
Orders for detrainment will be issued shortly.

6. Completion of relief will be wired and sent by runner to this Headquarters.

7. ACKNOWLEDGE.

                                                Captain,
                                        Brigade Major,
                                229th Infantry Brigade.

Issued at ....

Copies to :-

    Copy No.1 16th Devon Regt.
          2 12th Som.L.I.
          3 14th Rl.Highlrs.
          4 15th Suffolk Regt.
          5 229th L.T.M.Battery,
          6 'B' Coy. 74th M.G.Bn.
          7 H.Q., 74th (Yeo) Div.
          8 B.G.C.,229th Inf.Bde.
          9 War Diary
         10 File.

MARCH TABLE issued with 229th BRIGADE ORDER No. 78.

No.	Unit.	Relieved by.	To.	Guides.	Remarks.
1	15th Suffolks.	'A' Coy. & 'B' Coy. 1st Bn. American Regt.	Vicinity of FAUSTINE QUARRY.	1 per American platoon, and 1 per American Coy. H.Q. to be at the Cross Roads in F.30.d. at 8 p.m.	1 Officer will be sent in charge of each Battn. group of Guides.
2	14th Rl.Highlrs.	'C' Coy. 1st Bn. American Regt.	do	do	do
3	12th Som.L.I.	'D' Coy. 1st Bn. American Regt.	do	do	
4	16th Devon Regt.	'F' Coy. 2nd Bn. American Regt.	do	do	do

SECRET

ADMINISTRATIVE INSTRUCTIONS.

26th September 1918.

Reference this office No.58 of 26th instant :-

1. Captain J.F.SHELLEY, Royal 1st Devon Yeo. will act as entraining officer for Units of 229th Brigade Group. O.C.Units will send an entraining state to this officer at MERICOURT one half hour before the arrival of their unit.
Captain LEWIS, 24th Welsh Regt. will act as detraining officer for ~~the Brigade for~~ the Brigade Group at BERGUETTE.

2. <u>Supplies and Baggage Wagons.</u> Supply and Baggage Wagons of the Divisional Train will be entrained with Units to which they are affiliated and returned to the Train Companies after Refilling on the 29th instant.

3. <u>Supplies.</u> Rations for the 229th Brigade Group for consumption on the 29th instant will be drawn at MERICOURT at <u>9 a.m. 27th inst.</u> and will be taken on the train in the Supply Wagons after being drawn on the 27th instant.
   In order to avoid congestion, representatives of Units will be sent at the times stated above to take over these rations which will be loaded on to Supply Wagons after the rations for consumption 28th have been placed on the train.

4. Refilling Points on and after 29th instant for the 229th Infantry Brigade Group will be at HAM en ARTOIS at 11 a.m.

5. (a) One lorry will report at 229th L.T.M.Battery Hd.qrs. at 7 a.m. It will be loaded to ½ capacity only and returned forthwith to this Headquarters.
   (b) Blankets for battalions will be carried by train. Officers Commanding Battalions will send a guide to Brigade Hd.qrs. at 8.45 a.m. to guide lorries to Battalion Hd.Qrs. Blankets will be loaded without delay and be sent direct to MERICOURT and left under guard until departure of units. Lorries should be returned to M.T., Headquarters immediately after offloading at entraining station.

6. Sick from units entraining after the departure of Field Amb. on 27th and sick from units entraining 28th will be collected by 229th Field Amb. For this purpose O.C., 229th Field Amb. will leave behind one officer, one clerk, (with A.&.D.Book) one orderly as messenger, and three ambulances. Sick will be evacuated to C.C.S.PROYART.
   On the event of a motor ambulance being required at any of the entraining stations it can be had by telephoning to A.D.R.T., CORBIE. The motor ambulances are stationed in vicinity of his office.

7. Brigade Headquarters will close at 11 a.m. 27th instant. Exact location of Brigade Headquarters at destination will be notified on arrival of units at BERGUETTE.

Captain,
Brigade Major,
229th Infantry Brigade.

Copies to :-

16th Devons	12th Som.L.I.
14th Rl.Highlrs.	229th L.T.M.Battery
439th Fld.Coy.R.E.	448th Coy. A.S.C.
229th Field Amb.	S.A.A.Section D.A.C.
Capt. LEWIS,	Captain J.F.SHELLEY.

Secret.   Copy No 4

MEDICAL ARRANGEMENTS NO 12.
74th (Yeomanry) DIVISION.
Septr 26th 1918.

Reference Administrative Instructions relative to 74th Divn Order No 94

1.   Sick from units entraining after the departure of Field Ambulance on 27th and sick from units entraining 28th will be collected by 229th Field Ambulance.

       For this purpose O.C., 229 Field Ambulance will leave behind one officer, one clerk,(with A.&.D.Book) one orderly as messenger, and three ambulances. Sick will be evacuated to C.C.S. PROYART.

2.   On the event of a motor ambulance being required at any of the entraining stations it can be had by telephoning to A.D.R.T.,CORBIE. The motor ambulances are stationed in vicinity of his office.

3.   On completion of entrainment these motor ambulances will rejoin 229 Field Ambulance in the new area.

D.H.Q.   Colonel. A.M.S.
Issued at 7 p.m.   A.D.M.S., 74th(Yeo) Division.
Distribution. 3 Field Ambces
                3 Infy Bdes.
                "G" & "Q"
                C.R.E.
                A.D.R.T., Corbie.
                File.

SECRET.   Copy No.......

229th BRIGADE WARNING ORDER.

26th September 1918.

1. 229th Brigade Group will entrain at MERICOURT L'ABBE on 27th instant and detrain at BERGUETTE and proceed to HAM en ARTOIS Area where the Division will come under orders of G.O.C., XIII Corps in the Fifth Army.

2. March to Station will be by road through I.35.b., I.30.a. and c., Cross Roads J.21.a.

3. Full details follow.

4. ACKNOWLEDGE.

                                            J M Tuck
                                            Captain,
                                            Brigade Major,
                                            229th Infantry Brigade.

Issued at ....

Copies to :-

    Copy No. 1   16th Devon Regt.
         2   12th Som.L.I.
         3   14th Rl.Highlrs.
         4   229th L.T.M.Battery
         5   439th Fld.Coy. R.E.
         6   448th Coy. A.S.C.
         7   229th Field Ambulance
         8   S.A.A.Section, D.A.C.
         9   War Diary
        10   File.

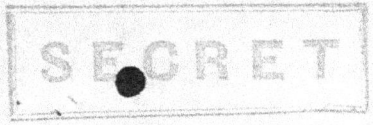

WARNING ORDER.

27th September 1918.

1. The 74th Division is relieving 19th Division in the line commencing probably on the night Oct. 2nd/3rd.

2. 19th Division holds roughly the old British Front line from S.23.a. to M.30.a. A plan of the present dispositions is being sent to you.

3. There are two Brigades in the line and one in Divisional Reserve. The front is roughly 6,000 yards.

4. Details of relief will be notified later.
    230th and 231st Brigades will be the Right and Left Brigades respectively in the line.

Lieut. Colonel,
General Staff.
74th (Yeomanry) Division.

Copies to:-
229th Infantry Brigade.
230th Infantry Brigade.
231st Infantry Brigade.
C.R.E.
'Q'.
74th Bn. M.G.C.
A.D.M.S.
74th Div. Train.

SECRET.

WARNING ORDER.

28th September 1918.

1. The 74th Division is relieving 19th Division in the line commencing probably on the night Oct.2nd/3rd.

2. 19th Division holds roughly the old British Front line from S.23.a. to M.30.a. A plan of the present dispositions is being sent to you.

3. There are two Brigades in the line and one in Divisional Reserve. The front is roughly 6,000 yards.

4. Details of relief will be notified later.
230th and 231st Brigades will be the Right and Left Brigades respectively in the line.

                                              Captain,
                                        Brigade Major,
                                  229th Infantry Brigade.

Copies to :-

    16th Devon Regt.
    12th Som.L.I.
    14th Rl.Highlrs.
    229th L.T.M.Battery,

SECRET

Copy No. 14

229th BRIGADE ORDER No.79.

September 29th 1918.

1. 74th Division will relieve 19th Division in the Line on nights 1st/2nd and 2nd/3rd October.

2. 229th Brigade Group will relieve 231st Brigade Group in Divisional Reserve (in new Sector) by light railway from BURBURE on October 2nd.

3. All transport will move by road, distances will be kept in accordance with Divisional March Standing Orders.

4. Completion of reliefs will be reported by wire or bicycle orderly to Brigade Headquarters which will be notified later.

5. All troops entering 19th Divisional Area will be under the Command of G.O.C., 19th Division until Command passes to G.O.C. 74th Division at 10 a.m. October 3rd.

6. Details as to times of Trains and move of Transport and Administrative Arrangements will be issued later.

7. ACKNOWLEDGE.

Captain,
Brigade Major,
229th Infantry Brigade.

Issued at 11 a.m.

Copies to :-

No. 1 B.G.C., 229th Infantry Bde.
2 16th Devon Regt.
3 12th Som.L.I.
4 14th Rl.Highlrs.
5 229th L.T.M.Battery
6 439th Field Coy.R.E.
7 229th Field Ambulance
8 448th Coy. Divl.Train
9 59th Mobile Vety.Section
10 H.Q., 74th (Yeo) Division.
11 Staff Captain
12 Bde.Signal Officer
13 Bde.Intelligence Officer
14 War Diary
15 File.

SECRET.

ADMINISTRATIVE INSTRUCTIONS
relative to 229th Brigade Order No. 79.

Sept. 30th 1918.

Trench and Area Stores.	1. All Trench and Area Stores will be taken over from outgoing units. Lists will be forwarded to this office by 8 p.m. on 3rd prox.
Dumps.	2. All dumps of R.E.Stores, S.A.A., Fireworks, Petrol tins, etc. will be taken over by relieving units. Lists giving the composition and location of each dump will be forwarded to this office by 8 p.m. on 3rd prox.
Baggage and Supply Wagons.	3. Baggage and Supply Wagons have been sent to report to units today. These will be retained until completion of the move and returned to the Train on 3rd prox.
Transport Lines.	4. Units will take over the transport lines of the units they relieve. These will not be altered when inter-Brigade reliefs take place.
Supplies.	5. (a) Rations for consumption 2nd Oct. will be drawn from BOURECQ at 7 a.m. on 1st Oct. (b) Rations for consumption 3rd Oct. will be drawn from BOURECQ at 7 a.m. on 2nd Oct. (c) Rations for consumption 4th Oct. will be drawn from X.13.a.0.6. at 9 a.m. on 3rd Oct.
Advance Parties.	6. Advance Billeting Parties will report at Brigade Headquarters, BOURECQ at 8 a.m. on 2nd October and be conveyed to new area by motor lorry.
Medical.	7. Medical Arrangements and locations of Field Ambulances in new area have already been issued direct to R.M.O's.

Captain,
Staff Captain,
229th Infantry Brigade.

Copies to :-

16th Devon Regt.
12th Som.L.I.
14th Rl.Highlrs.
229th L.T.M.Battery
229th Field Ambulance
439th Field Coy.R.E.
S.A.A.Section D.A.C.,
448th Coy. A.S.C.
59th Mobile Vety.Section.

SECRET.

229th BRIGADE WARNING ORDER.

Copy No......

Sept. 20th 1918.

1. 229th and 231st Brigades will attack and capture the Blue Line tomorrow Sept. 21st.
   Probable hour of Zero is 5 a.m.
   The Infantry forming up line and barrage start line are not yet settled and depend on success of operations of 12th Division which is now advancing and has reached QUENCHETTE'S WOOD.

2. Boundaries as follows :-

   Southern Divisional - F.20.c.7.8. - A.20.c.8.1.
      Not definite yet.

   Northern Divisional - F.25.c.3.3. - A.7.d.8.8.

   Between Brigades - F.29.b.7.5. - F.29.b.9.9. along bottom of CLAYMORE Valley in A.14.c.0.8.

3. 229th Brigade will hold the Green Line as follows :-

   16th Devons in Left Sector

   14th Rl.Highlrs. in Right Sector

   12th Som.L.I. in Brigade Reserve in TEMPLEUX QUARRIES.

   'B' Coy. 74th M.G.Bn. disposed for the defence of the Green Line.

   229th L.T.M.Battery - Two guns to each battalion in line, to be located in vicinity of PIMPLE Post and ORCHARD Post.

   1 Section 439th Fld.Coy.R.E. in TEMPLEUX QUARRIES.

   Headquarters 229th Brigade - FAUSTIN QUARRY, K.11.b.7.3.

   Battle Headquarters - TEMPLEUX QUARRIES.

4. (a) Lewis Gun Limbers will be kept ~~as near Battalion Hd.Qrs. as~~ in the vicinity of FAUSTINE QUARRIES possible.
   (b) Units will report forthwith location of Headquarters in order to facilitate finding communications.

5. There will be a conference of O.C.Units at Brigade Headquarters at 5 p.m. today.

                                        Captain,
                                        Brigade Major,
                                        229th Infantry Brigade.

Copies to :-

   B.G.C., 229th Inf.Bde.   'B' Coy. 74th M.G.Bn.
      16th Devon Regt.   1 Sect. 439th Fld.Coy.R.E.
      12th Som.L.I.   Staff Captain,
      14th Rl.Highlrs.   Intelligence Officer
      229th L.T.M.Battery   Bde.Signal Officer

Vol. 2.

Headquarters
229th Inf. Bde.
(74th Division)
October 1918

Headquarters,
    74th (Yeo) Division.

        Herewith War Diaries of this Brigade for the month of October.

                                                    Captain,
                                                  Brigade Major,
                                            for B.G.C. 229th Infty. Bde.
3-11-18.

Army Form C. 2118.

October 1918

Headquarters 229 I.B.

WAR DIARY
or
INTELLIGENCE SUMMARY
(Erase heading not required.)

Instructions regarding War Diaries and Intelligence Summaries are contained in F. S. Regs., Part II. and the Staff Manual respectively. Title Pages will be prepared in manuscript.

Place	Date Oct 1918	Hour	Summary of Events and Information	Remarks and references to Appendices
LECORNET	2nd		229th Brigade moved to a forward area in accordance with Brigade Order No 79 attached. Units were located as follows:- 229 Bde HQ. 229 L.T.M.B } LECORNET. 14 R.H. — LOCON 1/8 Gur. K.I. — ESSARS 16 Devons — HINGES	
PONTLOGY M.34.C	3rd		229th Brigade moved to an area W. of NEUVE CHAPELLE in accordance with order B.M.1 of 3.10.18 attached.	
T.4.a.1.7	4th		229 Brigade moved to an area W. of HERLIES in accordance with order B.M.2 of 3.10.18 attached. The relief of the enemy near Alochem and the line was held by 2/30 and 2/31 Brigades and 229 in Divisional Reserve. 229 Brigade infantry, were running and training was carried out.	
	5 - 10.58			
	Night 10/11		229 Brigade relieved the 2/31 Brigade in line accordance with Brigade Order No 81 attached. Preparations for further advance in the event of enemy withdrawal were made in accordance with Bde Order No 82 attached.	

2449 Wt. W14957/M90 750,000 1/16 J.B.C. & A. Forms/C.2118/12.

Army Form C. 2118.

WAR DIARY
or
INTELLIGENCE SUMMARY
(Erase heading not required.)

Place	Date	Hour	Summary of Events and Information	Remarks and references to Appendices
N 30 d 55	Night 14/15 Oct		14th RH relieved 12th SH in front line in accordance with Bde Order No. 83 attached	
	15th		Enemy reported to be withdrawing — in consequence 2/4 Bde advanced in accordance with Bde Order No. 84 attached. 14th RH who were Advanced Guard Bn. advanced our line about 3000 yards to line SANTES to LEZ HABOURDIN – further advance delayed owing to Brigade on left being unable to get on. Bde HQ moved to the Convent at O.28.a.	O.28.a.
O.28.a	16th		Advance to canal attempted but held up by enemy MGs about HABOURDIN and on canal bank. Line advanced about 1000 yards from yesterday. 16th Devons came through 12th SH & became support to Cotter going into Bde reserve. In the evening 16th Devons took over the left of the line, the line then being held by 2 battalions in depth & 1 in support on the line of the railway.	
	17th		In the early morning patrols found that the enemy were withdrawing – 16th Devons and 14th RH advanced to the line of the Canal DE LA HAUTE DEULE which it was found was still able to be crossed by infantry in file although bridge for transport had been destroyed. By midday 14th Devons & 14th RH were across the canal into HABOURDIN with patrols pushed out to the East. No enemy were seen or opposition encountered. By 1500 a pontoon bridge to carry transport was thrown over the canal. Orders were then issued for the advance to proceed – 16th Devons became Advanced Guard Battalion with 14th RH in support & 12th SH in reserve. The advance was continued until the advanced guard battalion reached an outpost line on the line of the railway East of RONCHIN, a distance of about 12,000 yards from the line held in the morning. 3000 due South of LILLE which was entered by our troops today. Brigade HQ moved to LA CROISETTE Q.26.a.	

WAR DIARY or INTELLIGENCE SUMMARY

Army Form C. 2118.

Place	Date	Hour	Summary of Events and Information	Remarks and references to Appendices
Q 26 c.	18th		Advance was continued at 0600. Cap A Coy to heavy fog in the morning advance was slow. At ASCQ enemy patrols were encountered. These retired before our advance but the enemy were found to be holding the East bank of the river LA MARCQ. We took up an outpost line in the line of the railway west of the river & carried out active patrolling especially towards the bridge at PONT A TRESSIN. As the advance on our left had not kept up with us, the 12th S.L.I. took up a line from HELLEMMES to ASCQ for the day & withdrew to ASCQ at dark when the 57th Bde came up on our left. Bde HQrs were established at the Rifle Range R 20 c for the day & moved to LEZENNES in the evening.	
LEZENNES	19th		Enemy had withdrawn during night 18/19th and 16th Dragoons crossed the MARCQ by the bridge at PONT A TRESSIN and took up an outpost line through CHERING. Orders had been issued that there would be no further advance today, but in consequence of the enemy withdrawal & the advance of the Division on our left orders were issued in the afternoon for the advance to proceed. 12th S.L.I. passed through 16th Dragoons & became Advanced Guard Battalion with 14th T.M.H. in support while 16th Dragoons remained on the line & came into Brigade reserve. The advance proceeded to a line running N & S through BRISSIEUX. Bde HQ moved to CHATEAU at PONT A TRESSIN.	
PONT A TRESSIN	20th		The advance was continued at 0800. Mounted patrols preceded the advanced guard battalion & encountered the enemy in MARQUAIN and its outskirts. Late in the day MARQUAIN was occupied by us, our front line running N & S, slightly East of MARQUAIN. Bde then moved from PONT A TRESSIN to Customs House at O 26 b 24.	

WAR DIARY or INTELLIGENCE SUMMARY

Army Form C. 2118.

(Erase heading not required.)

Place	Date	Hour	Summary of Events and Information	Remarks and references to Appendices
020d 24	21st		Our advance was held up most of the day by enemy machine guns from ORCQ and from the high ground to north. In the afternoon the 12th S.I. advanced on their right and were in position outside of ORCQ. After dark 12th S.I. made a general advance and reached a line of N.&S. through the Eastern outskirts of ORCQ. Further advance was checked by enemy determined m.g. fire.	
	22nd		The line reached by 12th S.I. on previous night was held by them during the day. After dark the 14th R.H. took over the front line with orders to advance to the road about 500 yards further East of possible push out patrols towards the canal bridge at Nord and of TOURNAI. Owing to the discovery of belts of wire in front of the enemy line no advance was made but the line was patrolled so as to get information for further advance. The enemy had many m.g. & t.m. in position here and were making a strong resistance.	
	23rd		No advance was made on the general line owing to the strength of the enemy defences. An effort was made to advance the right of our line so as to secure the flank of the Bde on our left right. One company of 14th R.H. attacked after a 10 minutes artillery, m.g. & t.m. bombardment & got to within 50 yards of their objective when they were driven back by intense enemy m.g. fire from the flanks & especially from the neighborhood of FAUBG DE LILLE. 6 killed & 29 wounded and our line then came back to the place from where the attack had started. During the night the

Army Form C. 2118.

WAR DIARY
or
INTELLIGENCE SUMMARY.
(Erase heading not required.)

Instructions regarding War Diaries and Intelligence
Summaries are contained in F. S. Regs., Part II.
and the Staff Manual respectively. Title pages
will be prepared in manuscript.

Place	Date	Hour	Summary of Events and Information	Remarks and references to Appendices
O20 d 24	24		Line was patrolled but at all points the enemy were found to be holding the line of the road with numerous machine guns. The advance was made to-day, enemy still holding on to west of TOURNAI. The 229 Bde. group was relieved in the line to-night 24th/25th in accordance with Bde. Order No. 85 (and coming under Divisional Reserve) attached, Bde. Hqrs moved to the Chateau at LUCHIN. (M36 a.)	
LUCHIN (M 36 a)	25		Instructions for the Defence of the present Divisional Front were issued and units instructed accordingly to reconnoitre the Main Line of Resistance. Bde. Order No. 86 (copy attached) was issued giving arrangements & march table for the advance of the Bde. in the event of the enemy withdrawing from TOURNAI. Bde. Units instructed to submit programmes of training including the following subjects:- Platoon Drill, Guard Mounting & Saluting Drill, Specialist Training, Map reading & writing of reports for NCOs & junior officers.	
26-31st			Training & S. detailed above was carried out by units of the 229 Inf. Bde. Bde. held its with increased [...] (Capt. & Adjt.) J. th Bde. group	

H.Q. 229 Inf. Bde.

J.M. [...]
Captain
Brigade Major

SECRET.

Reference Brigade Order No.79.

October 1st 1918.

1. Personnel of 229th Brigade Group will move by train from BURBURE (U.28.a.8.9.) at 2.30 p.m. on October 2nd in accordance with attached table.

2. All troops will arrive at the station by 2 p.m. and entrainment states will be handed to a representative from Brigade at 1.30 p.m.

3. Transport will move under Lieut T.HAWKINS, M.C., 12th Bn. Somerset Light Inf.

4. Completion of move to be reported by wire or bicycle orderly.

5. Brigade Headquarters will close at BOURECQ at 1 p.m. October 2nd, and open simultaneously at LONG CORNET (W.23.b.)

6. ACKNOWLEDGE.

Captain,
Brigade Major,
229th Infantry Brigade.

Copies to :-

B.G.C., 229th Infantry Brigade,
16th Devon Regt.
12th Som.L.I.
14th Rl.Highlrs.
229th L.T.M.Battery
439th Fld.Coy.R.E.
229th Field Amb.
448th Coy.A.S.C.
H.Q., 74th (Yeo) Div.
H.Q., 231st Infantry Bde.
Staff Captain
Bde.Signal Officer
Bde.Intelligence Officer
Bde.Supply Officer
Lieut HAWKINS,
War Diary,
File.

Route for Transport to destinations.

BAS RIEUX - BUSNETTES - GONNEHEM - HINGHES thence

No.	Unit.	From.	To.	Point of Detrainment.	Taking over from.	Transport Starting Point.	Pass Starting Point.
1	Bde.Hd.Qrs.	BOURECQ	LONG CORNET (W.23.b.)	)	231st Bde.Hd.Qrs.		10.30 a.m.
2	229th L.T.M.B.	BOURECQ	LONG CORNET (W.23.c.95.85.)	About W.17.	231st L.T.M.B.		
3	16th Devon Regt.	HAM en ARTOIS.	HINGES.	)	25th R.W.F.	Road Junction	10.32 a.m.
4	14th Rl.Highlrs.	BOURECQ	LOCON	)	24th Welsh.		
5	439th Fld.Coy. R.E.	BOURECQ	X.2.d.5.0.	About X.7.	94th Fld.Coy.R.E.	U.17.b.5.0.	10.42 a.m.
6	12th Som.L.I.	MANQUEVILLE.	ESSARS.	X.16.c.8.8.	10th K.S.L.I.		10.47 a.m.
7	229th Fld.Amb.	La FLANDRIE	BETHUNE (Brewery)	See Note x			10.37 a.m.

Note - x. Will be notified on arrival of Unit at BURBURE.

"A" Form
MESSAGES AND SIGNALS.

Army Form C. 2121
(In pads of 100.)

No. of Message............

Prefix.........Code..........m.	Words	Charge.	This message is on a/c of :	Recd. at......m.
Office of Origin an Service Instructions	Sent			
....	At ....m.		...................Service.	Date............
....	To			From ....
....	By		(Signature of "Franking Officer")	By..........

TO:
16th Devons
12th Som.L.I.
14th Rl.Highlrs.
229th L.T.M.B.

Sender's Number.	Day of Month.	In reply to Number.	AAA
BM 1.	3-10-18.		

229th	Brigade	will	~~move~~
forward	at	4.30	as
follows	aaa	Devons	to
~~Squares~~	~~S.15 and 16~~	~~route~~	via
LONG CORNET - ESSARS	aaa	Somersets
to	Squares	S.9,10 and	11
route	via	le TOURET	aaa
Black	Watch	~~to~~	~~M.29 and~~
30 and 35	route	via	LA CAUTORE
and	canal	crossings	in
X.8.b.	~~to~~	~~be~~	~~reconnoitred~~
at	once	aaa	Possible
Battn.	Hd.Qrs.	can	be
seen	~~in~~	location	maps
already	issued	aaa	Transport
will	move	with	units
aaa	Brigade	Headquarters	will
~~open~~	~~at~~	~~CURZON~~	~~POST~~
at	18.30	aaa	229th
L.T.M.B.	will	move	to
vicinity	of	new	Bde.Hd.Qrs.
all	reconnaissance will	be
made	forthwith	and	completion

From
Place
Time

The above may be forwarded as now corrected. (Z)
....
Censor.   Signature of Addressor or person authorised to telegraph in his name
* This line should be erased if not required.

"A" Form
MESSAGES AND SIGNALS.

Army Form C. 2121
(In pads of 100.)

of	moves	and	location
of	new	Btn.H.Q.	to
be	reported	to	Bde. H.Q.

From 229th Inf.Bde.

A.J.M.Tuck,
Capt.

"A" Form
MESSAGES AND SIGNALS.

Army Form C. 2121 (In pads of 100.)

No. of Message............

Prefix.......Code.......m.	Words	Charge.	This message is on a/c of :	Recd. at......m.
Office of Origin and Service Instructions	Sent		..................Service.	Date............
....	At ....m.			From ....
....	To			
....	By		(Signature of "Franking Officer")	By............

TO	16th Devons 12th Som.L.I. ~~14th Rl.Highlrs.~~		229th L.T.M.B.	
Sender's Number. BM.2	Day of Month. 3-10-18.	In reply to Number.	AAA	

Advance	of	Division	will
be	resumed	tomorrow	at
~~0800~~	aaa	1st	objective
U.22.b.	-	WAVRIN	0.29.cent.
- ERQUINGHEM	aaa	At	10.30
advance	will	~~be~~	~~made~~
to	2nd	objective	- line
of	canal	to	HAU
BOURDIN	thence	Northward	aaa
~~Bridge~~	~~Head~~	will	~~be~~
established	by	230th	Brigade
at	La	BLANCHE - des - SANTES	Line
aaa	~~Corps~~	~~Battle~~	~~Line~~
after	capture	of	2nd
objective	will	be	SAINGHIN
- BEAUCAMPS	- RADINGHEM aaa		~~Brigade~~
~~will~~	~~move~~	to	area
W. of	HERLIES	as	follows
aaa	Starting	Point	S.5.c.15.60
aaa	Pass	Starting	Point
Som.L.I.	at	0820	Devons
0837	R.H.	at	0854
L.T.M.B.	0911	aaa	Route

From ....
Place ....
Time ....

The above may be forwarded as now corrected. (Z)

....

Censor. Signature of Addressor or person authorised to telegraph in his name
* This line should be erased if not required.

Order No. 1625. Wt. W3253/   P 511. 27/2   H. & K., Ltd. (E. 2634).

"A" Form
MESSAGES AND SIGNALS.

Army Form C. 2121 (In pads of 100.)

will	be	LIGNY-le-PETIT	-
HALPEGARBE	Level	crossing	in
T.2.d.	to	destinations	as
follows	Som.L.I.	T.10.a. and b.	
and	T.4.c. and d.		South
of	HERLIES	-l'AVENTURE	(T.3.c.)
road	aaa	R.H.	T.4.a.
and b.	and	T.4.c. and d.	
N.	of	same	road
aaa	Devons	T.3.	North
of	same	road	aaa
Acknowledge			

From: 229th Inf. Bde
Place:
Time: 1430

(Z) A.I.M. Tuck,
Capt.

SECRET.

229th BRIGADE ORDER No. 80.

14 Copy No.

7th October 1918.

1. 229th Infantry Brigade will relieve the 231st Infantry Brigade in the Left Sector of the line on the night October 9th/10th in accordance with table attached.

2. All details of relief not mentioned in this order will be arranged between Battalion Commanders concerned.

3. Northern Divisional Boundary is altered to run from O.20.c.0.0. to P.11.a.6.3.
Inter Brigade Boundary is altered to run through Railway Junction at U.5.b.7.6.

4. 1 Officer per Bn.Hd.Qrs., 1 Officer per Coy. and 1 N.C.O. per Platoon of 229th Infantry Brigade will join Units to be relieved on the night 8/9th October.

5. Disposition Maps will be sent to this Headquarters by 6 p.m. on 10th instant.

6. Units of the 229th Infantry Brigade will NOT march through FOURNES when proceeding to the line.

7. All Aeroplane Photographs, Special Maps of Sector etc - will be handed over and receipts given.

8. B Teams of 229th Infantry Brigade will return to the Reception Camp under orders to be issued by the Staff Captain.

9. Completion of relief will be wired by Code Words "LOCATION RETURN".

10. Administrative Orders will be issued separately.

11. Location of Brigade Headquarters will be notified later.

12. ACKNOWLEDGE.

                                              Captain,
                                        Brigade Major,
                              229th Infantry Brigade.

Issued at 10 p.m.

Copies to :-

    No.1 B.G.C., 229th Infantry Brigade,
       2 16th Devon Regt.
       3 12th Som.L.I.
       4 14th Rl.Highlrs.
       5 H.Q., 74th (Yeo) Division
       6 229th L.T.M.Battery
       7 74th M.G.Bn.
       8 439th Fld.Coy.R.E.
       9 Bde.Supply Officer
     10 Staff Captain
     11 Intelligence Officer
     12 Bde. Signal Officer
     13 War Diary
     14 File.
     15. H.Q. 230 Inf Bde.
     16 H.Q. 231 Inf Bde.
     17 H.Q. 142 Inf Bde.

March Table issued with Brigade Order No. 80.

No.	Unit.	Relieving.	Hd.Qrs. at.	To.
1	14th Rl.Highlrs.	24th Welsh	O.26.d.6.1.	Left Subsection.
2	12th Som.L.I.	10th K.S.L.I.	U.2.b.7.7.	Right Subsection.
3	16th Devon Regt.	25th R.W.F.	U.1.b.1.7.	In Reserve.
4	229th L.T.M.Bty.	231st L.T.M.Bty.		

ADMINISTRATIVE INSTRUCTIONS

Relative to 229th BRIGADE ORDER No.80.

October 8th 1918.

1. **Trench and Area Stores.**

   All Trench and Area Stores including Packsaddlery, Petrol Tins, etc. surplus to Bn.Establishment will be taken over by Units from their corresponding unit of the 231st Infantry Brigade. Receipts will be given for them and lists of all such stores taken over will be forwarded to this office by 8 p.m. on 10th instant.

2. **Transport Lines.**

   Transport Lines and Q.M.Stores of 14th Rl.Highlrs. and 12th Som.L.I. will remain in their present positions. Transport Lines and Q.M.Stores of 16th Devon Regt. will move to vicinity of 12th Som.L.I.Lines on 9th instant.

3. **B Teams.**

   B Teams will proceed to 74th Division Reception Camp, LA BEUVRIERE tomorrow, 9th instant. They will report at Refilling Point, T.2.d.6.4. at 10 a.m. on 9th instant and proceed by empty Supply Lorries to CHOCQUES.

4. **Supplies.**

   Supplies will be drawn at same time and place as at present - i.e. T.2.d.6.4. at 0830. daily.

5. **Ammunition and R.E.Material.**

   Demands for S.A.A., Fireworks, and R.E.Material should reach this office by 1000 daily. The articles demanded will then be delivered at Units Transport Lines that day and sent up with the rations the same evening.

6. **Medical.**

   Car Loading Post for Left Sector will be at T.6.b.9.1. and the Advanced Dressing Station at HERLIES, T.4.d.9.9.

7. **Veterinary.**

   The Veterinary Officer in charge of Units of this Brigade is with the Mobile Vety.Section now located at N.32.a.3.7.

   Captain,
   Staff Captain,
   229th Infantry Brigade.

Copies to :-
   16th Devon Regt.
   12th Som.L.I.
   14th Rl.Highlrs.
   229th L.T.M.Battery
   439th Fld.Coy.R.E.

S E C R E T.
****

Copy No. 7
C.Q. 505/1

ADMINISTRATIVE INSTRUCTIONS RELATIVE TO
74th DIVISION ORDER No. 97.

1. The 231st Infantry Brigade will hand over to the 229th Infantry Brigade all Trench and Area Stores including, Packsaddles, Food Containers, and Petrol Tins.
    The 229th Infantry Brigade will forward to this office by the 12th inst, a list of the Stores taken over, signed by the Staff Captains of the two Brigades concerned.

2. The S.A.A. Section of the D.A.C. is located at T.2.a.1.9. All demands for S.A.A. and Fireworks will be made through Brigades and not by individual Units. The Orderlies attached to Brigades from the S.A.A. Section will invariably be used as Guides.

3. Transport Lines will not be exchanged. In future Transport Lines should be located so as to make it unnecessary to alter them on inter Brigade reliefs.

Headquarters.

8th October 1918.

[signature]
Lieut-Colonel
A.A. & Q.M.G.
74th (Yeo) Division.

Copies to :-

No.		No.	
1.	G.O.C.	11.	D.A.D.V.S.
2.	"G"	12.	Div. Train.
3.	3rd Corps.	13.	D.A.D.O.S.
4.	C.R.E.	14.	D.A.P.M.
5.	Signals.	15.	19th D.A.
6.	74th M.G.Battn.	16.	War Diary.
7.	229th Inf.Bde.	17.-18	File.
8.	230th Inf.Bde.	19.	Salvage Officer.
9.	231st Inf.Bde.	20-25	Spare.
10.	A.D.M.S.		

SECRET. WD. 229th BRIGADE ORDER No.81   Copy No. 16

8th October 1918.

1. Brigade Order No.80 is cancelled.

2. The Divisional and Brigade Boundaries are being readjusted as follows :-

   South Divisional Boundary
   Grid line between T.11 and T.17 (cross roads at T.11.c. inclusive to 55th Division) - T.12.c.0.0. - U.3.c.0.0. - Grid line East between U.3. and U.9.

   North Divisional Boundary
   O.20.c.0.0. - P.11.a.8.3. - P.11.b.8.3. - P.12.d.5.0. - P.14.c.0.8. thence eastward.

   Inter Brigade Boundary.
   O.31.d.2.4. - O.34.b.9.4. (road junction inclusive to Right Brigade) - P.27.a.0.0. - thence eastward.

3. On the night October 10th/11th the following reliefs will take place :-
   (a) 230th Infantry Brigade will relieve 231st Infantry Brigade as far North as Inter Brigade Boundary.
   (b) 229th Infantry Brigade will relieve 231st Infantry Brigade from new Inter Brigade Boundary to Northern Divisional Boundary.

4. 229th Infantry Brigade will be disposed in depth as follows :-
   (a) 12th Som.L.I. in line who will relieve 24th Welsh and portion of 10th K.S.L.I. North of new Inter Brigade Boundary, with Bn.Hd.Qrs. at O.26.d.5.1. All details of relief will be arranged direct between Commanding Officers concerned.
   (b) 14th Rl.Highlrs. in Support in vicinity of PETIT HAU BOURDIN, with joint Bn.Hd.Qrs. with 12th Som.L.I. Failing this Hd.Qrs. to be as near O.26.d.5.1. as possible. *(Move to be complete as soon as possible after dark.)*
   (c) 16th Devon Regt. in Brigade Reserve in N.30. and O.25.a. and c. Bn.Hd.Qrs. in N.30.b. *Move to be complete by 6 p.m.*
   Reconnaissance of the above locations will be made tomorrow, 9th instant.

5. Brigade Headquarters will close at 5 p.m. on 10th inst. and reopen at the same hour at N.30.d.5.5.

6. (a) The Corps Battle Line on completion of above readjustment will be a line running E.of FOURNES to BAS-FLANDRE.
   (b) The Outpost Line of Resistance will be the general line CARNOYE Farm - O.26.b.

7. 1 Officer from Bn.Hd.Qrs., 1 officer per Coy.Hd.Qrs. and 1 N.C.O. per Platoon from 12th Som.L.I. will join Units to be relieved on the night 9/10th October.

8. Disposition Maps will be sent to reach Brigade Headquarters by 6 p.m. on 11th instant.

9. All Aeroplane Photographs, Special Maps of Sector etc. will be handed over and receipts given.

10. Completion of relief will be wired by Code Words "LOCATION RETURN".

11. ACKNOWLEDGE.

Issued at ....10 p.m......

Jn Tuck
Captain,
Brigade Major,
229th Infantry Brigade.

Copies to :-

Distribution over/

Copies to :-

- No. 1 B.G.C., 229th Infantry Brigade,
- 2 16th Devon Regt.
- 3 12th Som.L.I.
- 4 14th Rl.Highlrs.
- 5 H.Q., 74th (Yeo) Division,
- 6 H.Q., 230th Infantry Brigade
- 7 H.Q., 231st Infantry Brigade
- 8 H.Q., 142nd Infantry Brigade,
- 9 229th L.T.M.Battery
- 10 74th M.G.Bn.
- 11 439th Fld.Coy.R.E.
- 12 Bde.Supply Officer,
- 13 Staff Captain,
- 14 Intelligence Officer
- 15 Bde.Signal Officer
- 16 War Diary
- 17 File.

SECRET

AMENDMENT to 229th BRIGADE ORDER No.81
dated 8th October 1918.
10-10-18.

1. The Northern Divisional Boundary as given in Brigade Order No.81 is altered and will now run from East to West as follows :-

    R.13.central thence East and West Grid Line to Q.16.a.6.0., Q.22.a.5.8., Q.15.c.6.3., Q.15.c.4.1., Q.14.d.5.5., Q.14.d.3.2., Q.14.c.2.3., Q.14.c.2.5., P.18.d.2.4., thence along Western edge of road to P.11.b.6.2., P.11.a.8.4., P.10.c.0.5., P.13.c.0.6., O.22.central., O.20.d.9.1., thence as before.

2. O.C., 12th Som.L.I. will arrange to take over the line from the Inter Brigade Boundary (which remains as shown in Brigade Order No.81) as far North as this Northern Divisional Boundary on the night 10/11th instant.

                                                 Captain,
                                        for Brigade Major,
                                   229th Infantry Brigade.

Copies to :-
    16th Devon Regt.
    12th Som.L.I.
    14th Rl.Highlrs.
    229th L.T.M.Battery
    H.Q., 142nd Inf.Bde.
    Bde.Signal Officer
    Bde.Intelligence Officer
    H.Q., 231st Infantry Brigade.
    File.

SECRET

AMENDMENT to 229th BRIGADE ORDER No.81
dated 8th October 1918.

10-10-18.

1. The Northern Divisional Boundary as given in Brigade Order No.81 is altered and will now run from East to West as follows :-

    R.13.central thence East and West Grid Line to Q.16.a.6.0., Q.22.a.5.8., Q.15.c.6.3., Q.15.c.4.1., Q.14.d.5.5., Q.14.d.3.2., Q.14.c.2.3., Q.14.c.2.5., P.18.d.2.4., thence along Western edge of road to P.11.b.6.2., P.11.a.8.4., P.10.c.0.5., P.13.c.0.6., O.22.central., O.20.d.9.1., thence as before.

2. O.C.,12th Som.L.I. will arrange to take over the line from the Inter Brigade Boundary (which remains as shown in Brigade Order No.81) as far North as this Northern Divisional Boundary on the night 10/11th instant.

                                     Captain,
                                for Brigade Major,
                                229th Infantry Brigade.

Copies to :-
    16th Devon Regt.
    12th Som.L.I.
    14th Rl.Highlrs.
    229th L.T.M.Battery
    H.Q., 142nd Inf.Bde.
    Bde.Signal Officer
    Bde.Intelligence Officer
    H.Q., 231st Infantry Brigade.
    File.

SECRET.   WD   Copy No......

Ref.Sheet 36 S.E.   229th BRIGADE ORDER No.82.
    Sheet 36 S.E.   10th October 1918.

1. In order to take prompt advantage of any further withdrawal by
   the enemy, the 229th Infantry Brigade Group will be prepared to
   advance under an Advance Guard constituted as follows :-

            Advance Guard Commander, O.C., 12th Som.L.I.
                12th Bn.Somerset Light Inf.
                1 18 pr.Battery to be detailed by O.C.
                    Left Artillery Group, 19th Div.
                1 Mobile 6" Newton T.M. to be detailed
                    by C.R.A., 19th Division.
                1 section 74th M.G.Bn. to be detailed by
                    O.C.,Left Coy. 74th M.G.Bn.
                1 section 432nd Fld.Coy. R.E. (This section
                    will revert to the order of the C.R.E.
                    immediately the Field Coys. arrive at
                    the canal and commence bridging)

   Immediately on an advance being ordered Commanders of Units
   composing the Advance Guard will report to O.C.,Advance Guard
   at 12th Som.L.I.Headquarters in O.32.b.8.9.

2. The advance will be made by the 229th Infantry Brigade Group in
   a series of bounds, each objective being made good before the
   Advance Guard proceeds to the next one.
   The first objective will be the general line V.1.d.0.0. - ROBOIR
   - SANTES - O.24.central - LEZ HAUBOURDIN.
   The second objective the line of the CANAL DE LA HAUTE-DEULE
   from LA PLANCHE DES SANTES to HAUBOURDIN and thence along the
   stream to BOIS DE L'ABBAYE.
   In the event of an advance to a third objective, the 12th Som.L.I.
/. will remain on the second objective and the 14th Rl.Highlrs will
   go through and become Advance Guard Battalion. Command of the
   Advance Guard will then pass to O.C.,14th Rl.Highlrs.

3. Advantage will be taken of any opportunity to establish small
   bridgeheads East of the CANAL. The Advance Guard Batteries must
   be prepared to cross the CANAL with any material locally obtain-
   able should it be found necessary to push detachments on further
   East to the high ground about Q.25.

4. Vigorous patrolling will be carried out by day and night along
   the whole Divisional front to keep in touch with the enemy in
   order to seize every opportunity of pushing forward immediately
   the enemy's resistance weakens.

5. In the event of the enemy retiring East of LILLE, the action of
   the right Division of the XIth Corps will be as follows.
   The 47th Division is to detach a force not exceeding one
   Infantry Brigade Group to secure the Southern and South-eastern
   exits of LILLE, and to maintain touch with the 74th Division.
   The route proposed for this detachment is via LE MARAIS (P.4.)
   - LOOS (P.18) - FAUBOURG DES POSTES (Q.13.& 14) to PORTE DE
   DOUAI (Q.22.a.)
   The action of the 55th Division will be similar to that of the
   74th Division.

                                                            s./

6. Troops will be warned of the necessity for lighting flares or for exhibiting tin discs or white flaps whenever aeroplanes sound their Klaxon Horns.

7. ACKNOWLEDGE.

                                                    Captain,
                                      for Brigade Major,
Issued at 0115   229th Infantry Brigade.

Copies to :-

    No.1 B.G.C., 229th Infantry Brigade
       2 16th Devon Regt.
       3 12th Som.L.I.
       4 14th Bl.Highlrs.
       5 229th L.T.M.Battery
       6 O.C., Left Coy.74th M.G.Bn.
       7 Section 439th Fld.Coy.R.E.
       8 O.C., Left Artillery Group,18th Div.
       9 H.Q., 74th (Yeo) Division
     10 H.Q., 230th Infantry Brigade
     11 H.Q., 142nd Infantry Brigade
     12 Bde.Signal Officer
     13 Bde.Intelligence Officer
     14 War Diary
     15 File.

SECRET

Headquarters,
  229th Infantry Brigade.
  230th Infantry Brigade.
  231st Infantry Brigade.
C.R.A. for information.

    Schemes of Brigades should reach this office 48 hours after receipt of this letter. Similarly Brigades should receive the schemes of Battalions and Battalions those of Companies and Companies those of platoons within 48 hours of the receipt of the order.

10th October 1918.

Lieut-Colonel,
General Staff,
74th (Yeomanry) Division.

SECRET.
****

SMALL LOCAL OPERATIONS.

BRIGADE OPERATIONS.

1. Each Infantry Brigade will prepare two schemes and make all arrangements to carry out two minor operations on their respective fronts.
   The 231st Infantry Brigade will either take over the plans of 230th Infantry Brigade or will prepare fresh plans.

BATTALION OPERATIONS.

Each Battalion will similarly prepare two schemes on the above lines and will be prepared to carry them out at 12 hours notice.

COMPANY OPERATIONS.

Each Company will prepare one scheme and will be prepared to carry the scheme into effect at 12 hours notice.

PLATOON RAIDS.

Each platoon Commander will select an enemy post which he considers he can successfully raid and will thoroughly explain his plans to his platoon. He will be ready at any time that an identification is required by the higher Command to produce a sample.
Not more than 2 samples are required from any one raid.

2. Conditions have arisen which render it imperative that the enemy should have no rest from our aggressive action. Divisions and lower formations may be called upon at from 24 to 6 hours notice to carry out certain offensive operations in order to

   (i) Improve the existing line.
   (ii) Obtain identifications.
   (iii) Harass the enemy.
   (iv) Maintain close touch to prevent an unimpeded withdrawal and to retain as much enemy strength as possible on the Divisional front.

   With these objects in view the enemy will be given no respite. His moral at the present moment is shattered and it must be a point of honour with the Division that full advantage is taken of this condition.

3. Yesterday a regrettable incident took place which is a slur upon the good name of the Division - namely that the enemy were allowed to make a successful raid upon one of our posts.
   The Divisional Commander knows that when he appeals to all ranks to wipe out this insult that he will not appeal in vain. 24 of our men are missing, ~~tonight~~ - the reply is obvious - 240 of the enemy alive or dead is that reply and only when that number is reached will he consider that they have been avenged.
   B.Gs.C. will take such steps as they consider desirable to convey the sentiments of the Divisional Commander to Battalions.

- 2 -

An operation will be carried out nightly on the Divisional front.

Full reports of the result of each operation will be rendered to Divisional H.Q. as soon as possible after it has taken place.

Stroud

10/10/18.

Lieut-Colonel,
General Staff,
74th (Yeomanry) Division.

SECRET.   W.D.

229th BRIGADE ORDER No.83.

Ref.Sheet 36.S.W.
1/20,000.

Copy No. 14

13th October 1918.

1. 14th Royal Highlanders will relieve 12th Som.L.I. in the Outpost Line on the night of 14th/15th instant. Move will take place as soon as possible after dark.

2. 12th Som.L.I. on relief will occupy the Outpost Line of Resistance, taking over the area now occupied by 14th Royal Highlanders.

3. All details of relief will be arranged between Commanding Officers concerned.

4. Trench Maps and Photographs dealing with the front line, and all Trench Stores will be handed over by 12th Som. L.I. to 14th Rl.Highlrs.

5. Completion of relief will be wired by following Code Word "FRENCH".

6. 16th Devon Regt. will remain in their present position.

7. ACKNOWLEDGE.

C.Mackintosh

Issued at 1300

Captain,
for Brigade Major,
229th Infantry Brigade.

Copies to :-
No. 1 B.G.C., 229th Infantry Brigade
    2 16th Devon Regt.
    3 12th Som.L.I.
    4 14th Rl.Highlrs.
    5 229th L.T.M.Battery
    6 H.Q., 74th (Yeo) Division
    7 H.Q., 230th Infantry Brigade
    8 H.Q., 162nd Infantry Brigade
    9 'C' Coy. 74th M.G.Bn.
   10 439th Fld.Coy.R.E.
   11 229th Bde.Signal Officer
   12   "   "   Intelligence Officer
   13 Staff Captain.
   14 War Diary
   15 File.

SECRET.

Ref.1/20,000 Map
Sheets 36 S.W.
36 S.E.

229th BRIGADE ORDER No. 84.

Copy No. 16.

15th
14th October 1918.

1. Information has been received from ~~prisoners~~ and patrols that the enemy is withdrawing on our front.

2. 229th Infantry Brigade Group will advance to the objectives laid down in para 2 of Brigade Order No.82 in accordance with the attached March Table.

3. O.C.Advanced Guard immediately on his arrival at the first objective will push forward patrols and exploit the ground to his front but will not leave the line of the first objective until receipt of further orders.

4. Transport (less Lewis Gun, Machine Gun, Trench Mortar, and R.F.limbers - which will accompany units) will be brigaded and march under Lieut HAWKINS, 12th Som.L.I. in rear of the column in the order of units on the march.

5. Brigade Headquarters will close at N.30.d.5.5. at Zero + 2 hours and reopen at the Convent O.22.c.4.0. at the same hour.

6. Zero Hour will be notified by wire.

7. ACKNOWLEDGE.

C Mackintosh
Captain,
for Brigade Major,
229th Infantry Brigade.

Issued at 0730 by Runner.

Copies to :-

No. 1 B.G.C.,229th Infantry Brigade,
2 16th Devon Regt.
3 12th Som.L.I.
4 14th Rl.Highlrs.
5 229th L.T.M.Battery
6 230th Infantry Brigade
7 142nd Infantry Brigade
8 74th (Yeomanry) Division
9 Left Group,19th Div.Arty.
10 Section 439th Fld.Coy.R.E.
11 'C' Coy. 74th M.G.Bn.
12 Bde.Signal Officer
13 Bde.Intelligence Officer
14 Staff Captain
15 Lieut HAWKINS,
16 War Diary
17 File.

MARCH TABLE.

Units.	Starting Point.	Time to pass Starting Point.	Route.	Remarks.
Advanced Guard O.C., 14/R.N. in Command 4" Royal Highlanders 4"2 Battery, R.F.A. 1 Section C.Coy. 74th M.G.Bn. 1 Section 439th Fld. Coy. R.E. 1 Mobile 3" Newton T.M.	Will start immediately on receipt of orders from this office, and will advance under dispositions as ordered by O.C. Advanced Guard.	ZERO		Section 439th Fld.Coy.R.E. will revert to orders of C.R.E. on reaching 2nd objective.
Main Body in Order of March.				
1st Somerset L.I.	Road Junction in 0.23.a.16.15.	Zero + 30	HAUTE DU FRULLE Cross Roads in 0.24.c.20.35. thence S.E. to Cross Roads in 0.24.c.5.4. thence N.E. along road to HAUCOURIN.	As the time for the Main Body to pass the Starting Point will depend on the rate at which the Advanced Guard is able to advance, the time Zero + 30 is only approximate, and will be altered at discretion of O.C. 1st Somerset L.I. The starting times of the remaining units will then be altered proportionally.
C.Coy.74th M.G.Bn. (less 1 Section)	"	Zero + 37	"	
229th T.M.Battery	"	Zero + 41	"	
16th Devon Regt.	"	Zero + 43	"	
Brigaded Transport.	"	Zero + 50	"	Baggage and Supply Wagons will march with each Unit's transport.

SECRET WD   Copy No. 19

229th BRIGADE ORDER No. 25

Ref. Map Sheet 37   23rd October 1918.
1/40,000.

1. The 229th Infantry Brigade will be relieved in the line by the 230th Infantry Brigade tonight 23rd/24th instant, as follows :-

    16th Devons   by   15th Suffolks
    12th Som.L.I.   by   16th Sussex
    14th Rl.Highlrs.   by   10th Buffs
    229th L.T.M.B.   by   230th L.T.M.B.

2. C.Coy.M.G.Bn. and Section 439th Fld.Coy.R.E. will remain attached to this Brigade.

3. On relief units will be disposed in billets as follows :-

    Bde.Hd.Qrs.   -   Chateau d'ESCANIN,   N.19.a.5.0.
    16th Devons   -   PAISIEUX, Hd.Qrs. at N.19.c.9.3.
    12th Som.L.I.   -   CAMPHIN, Hd.Qrs. at N.31.a.5.4.
    14th Rl.Highlrs.   -   PAISIEUX, Hd.Qrs. at N.19.c.1.0.
    229th L.T.M.B.   -   PAISIEUX, Hd.Qrs. at N.19.a.35.00.
    C.Coy.M.G.Bn.   -   CAMPHIN, Hd.Qrs. at N.31.a.6.4.
    439 Fld.Coy.R.E.   -   TRIEU - MAZERELLE,   N.20.a.

4. The troop King Edward's Horse at present attached to this Brigade will be transferred to the 230th Infantry Brigade.

5. Artillery reliefs are being arranged separately by C.R.A.

6. All details of relief not provided for in this order will be arranged direct between Commanding Officers concerned.

7. Completion of relief will be wired to this office using as Code Words the name of the Commanding Officer concerned.

8. ACKNOWLEDGE.

                                            C.Mackintosh
                                            Captain,
                                            for Brigade Major,
Issued at ....   229th Infantry Brigade.

Copies to :-

    No.1 R.G.C.,229th Inf.Bde.   No.10 74th (Yeo) Division
       2 16th Devons   11 104th Infantry Brigade
       3 12th Som.L.I.   12 171st Infantry Brigade
       4 14th Rl.Highlrs.   13 230th Infantry Brigade
       5 229th L.T.M.Battery   14 231st Infantry Brigade
       6 C.Coy.74th M.G.Bn.   15 Brigade Supply Officer
       7 439th Fld.Coy.R.E.   16 Staff Captain
       8 Left Artillery Group,   17 Brigade Signal Officer
       9 O.C.,Troop K.E.H.   18 Brigade Intelligence Officer
                                         19 War Diary
                                         20 File.

Copy No. 18

SECRET   229 Infantry Brigade Order No. 86.

Ref. MAP.   25th Oct 1918
Sheet 37 1/40,000.

1. INFORMATION.
   When the enemy retires the immediate objectives of the 230th Bde are:-
   (a) To cross the River ESCAUT by the bridges in O.23.a.
   (b) To form a bridgehead from WARCHIN (exclusive) to O.17 Central.
   (c) To capture RUMILLIES (P.15) keeping touch with 55th Division on the Railway P.16.c and with the 57th Division on high ground in P.9.c.
   (d) East of River ESCAUT the tactical Boundary between the 74th & 55 Divisions will be the Railway from P.19 Central to P.16.C.
   (e) The picquetting of the Town of TOURNAI is to be undertaken by the 231st Brigade.

2. The Field Artillery Brigade attached to 229 Inf Bde and "C" Coy 74th M.Gun B. have been temporarily placed at the disposal of 231st Bde for the defence of the Main Line of Resistance but will rejoin this Bde on the advance being resumed.

3. The 229 Bde Group will be prepared to advance in support of the 230th Bde, and on receipt of instructions giving ZERO hour for the advance will move off in accordance with the attached March Table.

4. Transport (Less L.G., M.G., & T.M. limbers which will accompany units) will be brigaded & march under command of LIEUT HAWKINS, 12 SOM. L.I., in order of units on the march.

5. Acknowledge.

Issued at 1800 By runner.

C Mackintosh Capt
for Bde Major
229 Inf Bde

Copy No 1. B.G.C.
2. 16. Divon.
3. 12 Som. L.I.
4. 14 R.H.
5. 229 T.M.B.
6. C. Coy M.G.B.
7. Bde R.F.A.
8. 439. Fd.C. RE.
9. Bde Signal Officer
10. " Int. Officer.
11. Staff Captain
12. Lieut Hawkins
13. 74th Divn.
14. 230. Inf Bde
15. 231. Inf. Bde
16. War Diary
17. File.
18. Spare.

MARCH TABLE.

UNIT.	STARTING POINT.	Time to pass starting point.	ROUTE.	REMARKS.
Bde. H.Q. & Sig. Section.	Rue R. fork on main BAISIEUX-TOURNAI road at N.2.D.C.3.4.	ZERO.	Main TOURNAI road through FAUBG DE LILLE to O28a a.39 thence N & E to Bridge at Q.23.a.o.6.	Lewis Gun, machine gun & Trench mortar limbers will accompany units on the march.
16th Devons.	"	ZERO + 2.	"	Brigade will halt for 10 minutes from 10 minutes before the clock hour to the clock hour.
Section 439 Fld F Coy R.E.	"	ZERO + 13	"	
"C" Coy M. Gun Bn.	"	ZERO + 16	"	Intervals between units on the march will be maintained as in 74th Div. Standing Orders & Amendments.
12. Somerset L.I.	"	ZERO + 20	"	
229. L.T.M. B+Y.	"	ZERO + 35	"	
14th R. HDRS.	"	ZERO + 37	"	
Bde. R.F.A.	"	ZERO + 62	"	Baggage & Supply wagons will march with the transport of the units to which they are affiliated.
Brigaded Transport in order of units on the march.	"	ZERO + 92	"	

SECRET.   Copy. No 19

REF MAP.   229 Infantry Brigade Order No 87.
Sheet 37 /40,000   31st Oct 1918.

1. Brigade Order No. 86. is cancelled, and the following substituted.

2. When the enemy retires, Brigade Groups will be formed and will be known as follows:—
   Advanced Brigade Group. - 231st Inf. Bde.
   TOURNAI Brigade Group - 230th " "
   and Divisional Reserve Brigade Group. (229th Inf Bde) which will be formed as follows:—

   16th Devons   179 (Army) Bde. R.F.A.
   12th Somerset L.I.   R.A.R.E. (Less 1. Section)
   14th R.H.   R.M.R.E (Less 1. Section)
   229. L.T.M.B.   Pioneer Bn (less 1. Coy)
   117th Bde. R.F.A.   Machine Gun Bn less.1.(Coy)

3. The immediate Objectives of the advanced Guard Bde are:-
   (a) To cross the river ESCAUT by the Bridges at O.23.a. O.6. and H.7.
   (b) To form a bridgehead from WARCHIN (exclusive) to O.17. Central.
   (c) To capture RUMILLIES (P.15.) keeping touch with the 55th Division on the Railway in P.16.c. and with the 57th Division on the high ground in P.9.c.
   after the capture of these objectives the Advanced Guard Bde. will be prepared to undertake any further operations if ordered.
   East of the River ESCAUT the Southern Divisional Boundary will be the railway from P.19. Central to P.16.c.

4. Further orders for the TOURNAI Brigade Group are in the attached appendix, forwarded to Battalions and L.T.M.B. only.

5. The 229 Bde Group will be prepared to advance in support of the 230th Bde, and on receipt of instructions giving ZERO hour for the advance will move off in accordance with the attached March table without further orders.

                                              6/ Infantry Transport

6. Infantry Transport of the Brigade (less L.G and T.M. limbers which will accompany Units) will be brigaded and march under command of LIEUT. HAWKINS. M.C. 12th Somerset L.I., in order of Units on the March.

7. Acknowledge.

Issued at 1530
By. D.R.L.S. & runner.

A.J.M. Tuck
Captn.
Brigade Major.
229th Inf Brigade.

Copies to:-
1. B.G.C.
2. O.C. 16th Devons
3. O.C. 12 Som. L.I
4. O.C. 14th B.H.
5. O.C. 229. L.T.M.B
6. O.C. 74th M. Gun Bn
7. O.C. R.M.R.E.
8. O.C. R.A.R.E
9. O.C. 1/12 Loyal. N. Lancs.
10. H.Q. 117. Bde R.F.A
11. H.Q. 179. A. Bde. R.F.A.
12. H.Q. 74th Yeo Divn.
13. H.Q. 230. Inf. Bde.
14. H.Q. 231. Inf. Bde
15. Lieut Hawkins M.C.
16. O.C. 229. Signals.
17. Bde. Intelligence Officer.
18. Staff. Captain.
19. War. Diary.
20. File.

MARCH TABLE.

to accompany 229 Infantry Brigade order No. 87.   31st Oct/1918

UNIT.	STARTING POINT.	Time to pass Starting point.	ROUTE.	REMARKS.
Bde. H.Q. and Signal Section.	Cross Roads in N.21.d.	Zero.	Main TOURNAI road through FROIDMONT to O.28.a.O.3. thence N.&.E. to Bridge at O.23.a.O.6.	Brigade Group will halt for 10 minutes from 10 minutes before the clock hour, to the clock hour. Time halts have been allowed for in times to pass Starting point.
16th Devons	"	ZERO + 2	"	
14th R.H.	"	ZERO + 17	"	
12th Somerset L.I.	"	ZERO + 32	"	Intervals between units on the march will be maintained as in 74th Div. Standing orders and Amendments.
229 L.T.M.B.	"	ZERO + 43	"	
M.Gun Bn.(Less I.Coy)	"	ZERO + 45	"	
R.M.R.E.(Less I.Sect.)	"	ZERO + 73	"	
R.A.R.E.(Less I.Sect.)	"	ZERO + 79	"	
Pioneer Bn.(Less I.Coy)	"	ZERO + 65	"	Baggage and Supply Waggons will march with the Transport of the units to which they are affiliated.
117 Bde. R.F.A	"	ZERO + 100	"	
179 A.Bde. R.F.A.	"	ZERO + 140	"	
Infantry Transport Less L.G and L.T. M.B. Limbers in order of units on the march.	"	ZERO + 170	"	

Vol. 8.

Headquarters,
229th Inf. Bde.
(74th Division)

November 1918.

Headquarters,

74th (Yeo) Division.

HEADQUARTERS
229th INFANTRY BDE.
Date 3-12-18
Ref. No. 47/2

Herewith War Diaries of Units of 229th Infantry Brigade for month of November 1918.

Through error 14th R.H. have forwarded Diary to 3rd Echelon.

3rd Decr. 1918.

Captain,
Brigade Major,
for Lieut Colonel,
Commanding 229th Infantry Bde.

Army Form C. 2118

WAR DIARY or **INTELLIGENCE SUMMARY**

(Erase heading not required.)

Map Reference Sheets 37 and 38. Scale 1/40,000.
Instructions regarding War Diaries and Intelligence Summaries are contained in F.S. Regs., Part II. and the Staff Manual respectively. Title Pages will be prepared in manuscript.

Headquarters, 229th INFANTRY BRIGADE.

Place	Date	Hour	Summary of Events and Information	Remarks and references to Appendices
CAMPHIN.	November 1st to 8th.		Platoon and Company Training continued.	
LAMAIN.	9th		Enemy resumed his Retreat and 229th Brigade Group moved forward in Support of 231st Brigade Group, and was located as follows :- Brigade Hd.Qrs.) 16th Devon Regt. = HERTAIN 229th L.T.M.Bty.) LAMAIN. 12th Som.L.I. = CAMPHIN 14th Rl.Highlrs.) M.G.Batt. = ORCQ 117th Bde. R.F.A.)	
LA ROSIERE FARM.Q.9.c.	10th		Advance continued in accordance with Brigade Order No.89 attached.	
CORNET B.25.d.	11th		Advance continued in accordance with Brigade Order No.90 attached. At 1040 hours was received that hostilities would cease at 1100, and no eastward movement would take place after that hour. All troops were halted and billeted, but at 1220 this order was cancelled by G.O.C.,Division and the forward movement was continued according to above order. Lieut.(T.Captain) A.H.GRANT, M.C., 3rd Bn.S.Lancashire Regt. took over the duties of Staff Captain from Lieut.(T.Captain) C.MACINTOSH, 4th Bn.The Royal Scots., posted as Staff Captain No.3 Tank Group.	
	12th		Advance continued in accordance with Brigade Order No.91 attached. The 229th Brigade Group passed through 231st Brigade Group and took up the ARMISTICE LINE as shown in above order.	
	17th		229th Brigade Group was relieved by 87th Brigade Group, and marched West, in accordance with Brigade Order No.92 attached. 117th Brigade left the Group. R.F.A.	18th/

Army Form C. 2118

WAR DIARY or INTELLIGENCE SUMMARY
(Erase heading not required.)

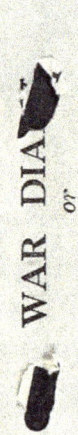

Place	Date	Hour	Summary of Events and Information	Remarks and references to Appendices
	November 18th.		16th Devon Regt. moved from BUISSENAL to PIPAIX, and the 12th Som.L.I. moved from MAINVAULT to L'UZE. M.G.Battalion left the Brigade Group. Brigadier General F.S.THACKERAY, D.S.O., M.C., proceeded on leave, and Lieut Colonel G.S.POOLE, D.S.O. took over Command of the Brigade in his absence.	
	19th.		Brigade Headquarters moved from MAINVAULT to L'UZE. 439th Field Coy. R.E. moved to BUISSENAL.	
	20th.		439th Field Coy. R.E. moved to HOUTAING	
	19th to 30th.		16th Devon Regt. and 12th Som.L.I. worked on the MAIN LINE (TOURNAI - BRUSSELS) Railway near their respective areas. 14th Royal Highlrs. did two days work on roads. The Education Scheme made great progress. The Division being divided into Groups for this purpose, and Group Classes were organized.	

Headquarters,
229th Infantry Brigade.
1st Dec.1918.

A.M. Tuck.
Captain,
Brigade Major,
229th Infantry Brigade.

WD

ADDENDUM to 229 Infantry Brigade
         Order No. 87.   Nov. 1st/18.

1. In order to test the enemy's strength and if possible to expedite his withdrawal, the 231st Brigade in conjunction with the 55th Division on our right, will conduct an operation tomorrow morning Nov. 2nd at 0515.

2. The action of the 231st Brigade will be confined to an intense bombardment followed by a barrage lifting from the enemy front-line system, to his second system, and at 0541 lifting off his second system, and patrols being sent forward along our entire front.

3. Should the patrols draw fire, they will return to our lines, but, if the enemy has retired, or shows signs of weakening, they will continue their advance and the Advance Guard Brigade will be set in motion.

4. In view of the above, the 229 Brigade will be held in readiness to move at short notice in accordance with Brigade Order No. 87, as modified below.

5. The 229 Brigade Group laid down in para. of Brigade Order No. 87 will not be formed.

6. The order of march as shown in the March Table issued with Brigade Order No. 87 will hold good for Units of the 229 Brigade, with the exception that Infantry Transport (less L.G and L.T.M.B limbers) will move in rear of 229. L.T.M.B and pass the Starting point Zero + 45 minutes.

7. In para 5 of Brigade Order No. 87, for 230th Bde. read 231st Brigade

8. Acknowledge.

Issued to all recipients of
Brigade Order No. 87.

                              Captn.
                         Brigade Major
                      229 Infantry Brigade

SECRET. FILE.   Copy No 19.

229 Infantry Brigade Order No 88.

REF MAP.
Sheet 37. S.W. 1/20,000.   7th 1700. 1918

1. 229th Infantry Brigade will relieve the 165th Infantry Brigade, 55th Division on Novr 8th and night 8th/9th Novr in accordance with attached table.

2. A Summary of information concerning the Sector to be relieved is forwarded separately (to Units of 229 Bde only) and a tracing showing dispositions attached for O.C. 12th Somerset L.I.

3. A map showing dispositions will be forwarded by all Units to this H.Q by 1800 on 9th inst.

4. All details not mentioned in this order will be arranged between Commanding Officers direct.

5. Completion of relief will be reported by wire using name of Commanding Officer concerned as Code word.

6. Administrative orders will be issued separately by the Staff Captain.

7. Bde. H.Q. will close at 1700 at Chateau de LUCHIN and reopen at the same hour at ESPLECHIN (T.10.d. 65, 25.)

8. To be acknowledged by addressees.

Issued at   by D.R.L.S
                  and runner.

Copies to
No. 1 O.C. 16. Devons   Bde Int Officer.
" 2   "   12 Som.L.I.   " Signal Officer
" 3   "   14 R.H   " Supply "
" 4   "   229 L.T.M.B.   448 Co. A.S.C
" 5   H.Q. 165. Inf Bde
" 6   "   Right Bde 55 Divn   Town Major
" 7   "   231 Inf. Bde   BAISIEUX
"   "   230   "   Area Commdt. CHERENG
"   "   74th Yeo. Div.   War Diary.
       B.G.C   File.
       Staff Capt.

a./f.M. 1 LICK

Captain.
Brigade Major.
229. Inf Bde.

MARCH TABLE.

To accompany 229th Infantry Brigade order No.S.S. Nov. 7th 1918.

UNIT.	FROM.	RELIEVING.	TO.	GUIDES at	ROUTE.	REMARKS.
4th Somerset L.I.	CAMPHIN.	6th King's	LINE.	Battalion H.Q. U.7.d.32.76	CREPLAINE.	Relief to be complete as soon after dark as possible.
4th DEVONS.	CHERENG.	7th King's	Support.	Battalion H.Q. T.4.a.7.4.	CAMPHIN CREPLAINE.	Relief to be complete by 1600.
4th ROYAL HIGHLANDERS.	GRUSON.	5th King's	Reserve FROID-MONT.	WEST edge of FROIDMONT.	CREPLAINE. ESPLECHIN.	Relief to be complete by 1600.
229 L.T.M.B.	CAMPHIN.	155th L.T.M.B			As arranged by O.C's. concerned.	

* Not ESPLECHIN as shown in Warning Order.

SECRET.

SUMMARY OF INFORMATION CONCERNING SECTION TO BE RELIEVED.

Reference Sheet 37 S.W. 1/20,000.

The following is the dispositions and role of Battalions of the Brigade:-

1. The PICQUET LINE is a general Line U.4.c. U.3.b. O.33. c and a. O.26.d.

    THE OUTPOST LINE OF RESISTANCE is a general line running U.R.& central. U.2.b and d central. O.32. central.

    THE MAIN LINE OF RESISTANCE will be on the line T.11.b.8.2 and East of the Road Junction on the high ground in N.36.c.05.15.

2. DISTRIBUTION OF BATTALIONS.

    'A' Battalion (Line) — Battalion Headquarters U.7.d.32.76.

        1 Company — Company H.Qrs. U.3.d.32.56 with posts in U.4.c U.3.b. U.3.d and U.2.d.

        1 Company — Company H.Qrs. U.1.d.60.75 with posts in O.33.c. O.33.a. O.32.a. O.26.c. O.32.d.

        1 Company — Company H.Qrs. U.7.b.80.10 with Company in billets at U.7.b and d. U.8.a.

        1 Company — Company H.Qrs. U.1.d.70.75. with Company in billets at U.2.b. and U.1.d.

    'B' Battalion (Support) — Battalion Headquarters T.4.a.70.40.

        1 Company — Company H.Qrs. T.11.b.35.40 with a series of posts on the general line T.11.b.8.2 to T.6.a.60.20.

        1 Company — Coy. H.Qrs. N.36.c.15.35 with a series of posts on the general line T.6.a.60.20 to N.36.c.70.90.

        1 Company — Coy. H.Qrs. N.35.c.75.75 with a series of posts on general line N.36.c.0.5. to N.35.d.0.9.

        1 Company — Coy. H.Qrs. N.34.d.00.50 with posts at T.5.a.8.6. T.5.b.30.30 N.35.c.9.0. N.35.c.60.35.

    'C' Battalion (Reserve) — Battalion H.Qrs. T.12.b.20.10. Battalion in billets in T.12.b.

3. ROLE OF BATTALIONS.

    'A' Battalion furnish the OUTPOSTS, i.e. manning the PICQUET LINE and the OUTPOST LINE OF RESISTANCE.
    (a). To locate and keep touch with the enemy.
    (b). To move forward and follow up the enemy the moment he shows signs of withdrawing, especially aiming for the bridge O.30.c.8.2.
    (c). To fight to the last if attacked, on the ground it is holding at the time of attack.

(d). To place examining posts on all roads leading East and West through the OUTPOST LINE OF RESISTANCE. It will be the duty of these posts to detain all civilians and soldiers unknown to them who pass along or near these roads until enquiry has been made as to their credentials. No civilians will be allowed to pass Eastwards along these roads.

'B' BATTALION will be disposed of in the MAIN LINE OF RESISTANCE, where it will remain and fight to the end.

'C' BATTALION in Brigade Reserve and will be used :-

   (a). To reinforce the Line of Resistance.
   (b). To counter-attack.

This Battalion will not move without orders from Brigade Headquarters.

4. MACHINE GUNS.

The Left Group of the Machine Gun Battalion is disposed as follows :-

8 Guns with the OUTPOST BATTALION.
8 Guns on the MAIN LINE OF RESISTANCE.
8 Guns in MOBILE RESERVE at FROIDMONT.

5. 5" STOKES GUNS.

Two are with the OUTPOST BATTALION. Six in MOBILE RESERVE.

6. FLANK BRIGADES.

   Right Brigade. OUTPOST LINE OF RESISTANCE is the general Line St.MAUR-Spur N.E. of BEAUREGARD Fm. - ERE.

RESERVE LINE to the OUTPOST LINE OF RESISTANCE is the general line MONT au GRIS - PIC au VENT Line.

MAIN LINE OF RESISTANCE is roughly a line running N and S immediately East of ESPLECHIN.

   Left Brigade.

OUTPOST LINE OF RESISTANCE runs O.26.c.0.0. - O.25.d.4.5 - O.25.b.3.3 - O.19.b.0.5 to junction with 57th Division at O.13.a.5.0.

MAIN LINE OF RESISTANCE runs approximately N.35.a.8.4 - N.29.d.6.0. - N.29.Central - N.23.c.9.1 - N.23.b.4.0 - N.17.d.8.0 - N.17.b.9.0 with a refused flank in N.17.b owing to MAIN LINE OF RESISTANCE of 57th Division being in advance of this line. Point of junction with Left Brigade on MAIN LINE OF RESISTANCE will be N.35.b.0.

Two Battalions are in the FRONT LINE and OUTPOST LINE OF RESISTANCE, one Battalion in RESERVE.

Forward Battalions have two Companies in the FRONT LINE and two Companies in the OUTPOST LINE OF RESISTANCE. Headquarters of all three Battalions are in MARQUAIN.

In case of attack the OUTPOST LINE OF RESISTANCE will be maintained by utilizing all available Brigade Reserves.

SECRET W.D   Copy No 11

229 Infantry Brigade Order No 89

Ref Sheet 37   Nov 9th 1918
Scale 1/40,000

1. The Advanced Guard Brigade will continue its advance on Nov 10th at 0800. The first objective will be high ground in R.14a and R.2. The second objective will be the Railway in R.12 and R.6.

2. Southern Divisional Boundary will now be ALTIERE - LA MOURETTE (both exclusive) - R.14.b.c.0.0.

3. 229 Brigade Group will move in accordance with March Table attached, to an area EAST of TOURNAI.

4. Billeting parties on Bicycles will meet the Staff Captain at Starting point (Shown in March Table) at 0800.

5. Transport will move with Units.

6. Brigade H.Q. will close at 0830 and after this hour reports will be sent to the head of the column. Brigade H.Q. will open on arrival at BECLERS.

7. Addressees to acknowledge.

C.S.M. Tuck
Captain,
Brigade Major.
229 Inf. Bde.

Issued at ......
By D.R.L.S. + Runner.
Addressed to:-
 O.C. 1 Devons
 " 12 Som. L.I.
 " 14th R.H.
 " 229 L.T.M.B.
 " 117 Bde. R.F.A
 " 74 M. Gun Bn.

Copies to:-
 B.G.C.
 Bde. Signalling Officer.
 " Intelligence
 H.Q. 74th Yeo Divn.
 War Diary.
 File.

MARCH TABLE.

Issued with Brigade order No 89.   Nov 9th 1918.

UNIT.	FROM.	TO	STARTING POINT	Time to Pass S.P.	ROUTE.	REMARKS.
Brigade H.Q. 229.L.T.M.B.	LAMAIN	THIMOUGIES-BECLERS-HAVINNES. AREA	Road Junction at N.30.a.9.4.	0900	FAUBOURG de LILLE - TOURNAI - crossing ESCAUT, by Ponts of FAUBOURG de MORELLE 029d 9.7 - FAUBOURG de RAMILLIES.	
16th DEVONS	HERTAIN			0903		
12th Som.L.I.	CAMPHIN			0920		Route to Starting Point via LAMAIN
14th R.H.	LAMAIN			0937		14th R.H. will not move off until 12.S.om.L.I. am ethon by Road Junction at N.29.c.8.7. 28
74th M.G.Bn. (less 1. Coy.)	H.Q. ORCQ 2.Coys. MARQUAIN 1.Coy. HERTAIN			1004		
117th Bde R.F.A.	LAMAIN			1026		

NOTE. Lewis Gun Limbers will march in rear of their Companies.
       Distances as laid down in Divisional Standing Orders for marches & for Transport.

SECRET   W.D.   Copy No. 11

229 Infantry Brigade Order No. 90.
Map Ref Sheet 37 & 38   Nov. 11th/18
Scale 1/40,000.

1. 229 Brigade Group will move East on Nov 11th in accordance with March Table attached. Billeting in depth EAST of a line through Gr. 7 Central.

2. Billeting parties on Bicycles will meet the Staff Captain at 0800 at the church in THIMOUGIES.

3. Refilling point will be at P.15.c.5.0. (Sheet 37) at 0500.

4. O.C. 117 Bde. R.F.A. will detail an orderly to meet No. 1 Section D.A.C. on arrival at FRASNES-LEZ-BUISSINELLES who will instruct No. 1 Section to proceed to POME (A 30 c.)

5. Brigade H.Q. will close at 0800 after this hour reports to be sent to the head of the Column. Brigade H.Q. will open on arrival at LAHAMAIDE.

6. The Brigade Group will halt from 1150 to 1300. All personnel and vehicles (if possible) to be clear of the road.

7. Addressees to acknowledge.

Issued at 0145...
By D.R. L.S. & runner.

Addressed to:-
1. O.C. 16 Devons.
2. " 12 Som L.I.
3. " 14 R.H.
4. " 229 L.T.M.B.
5. " 117 Bde. R.F.A.
6. " 7 M.G. Bn.

Copies:
B.G.C.
Staff Capt.
Bde Sig. Officer
Adjutant "
War Diary
FILE.

[signed] J. M. Tuck
Captain.
Brigade Major.
229 Inf. Bde.

To accompany Brigade Order No. 1:- Mar 11th 1918. REMARK 6.

UNIT.	STARTING POINT. FROM	TO	STARTING POINT Time to pass	ROUTE.	REMARK 6.
2nd H.Q. 29.LTMB	LA POSIERE. FARM. BECLERS	In an area between 67 Field (Sh.45/35) and LAHAMAIDE B.6/5/46 (Sh.35) CrossRoads in DIME (L.25.a.1.1.)	0900	DIME (L.25.n)– FRASNES·LEZ·BUISSENELLES– –LAHAMAIDE	Route to Starting point via MELLES and QUARTES.
15.DEVONS	THINIDOEIES		0903		Guide from 229th M.Coy join section D.A.C. in FRASNES LEZ BOUSSINELLES.
177 Bde R.F.A.	HAUT REJET Area.		0920		
74th M.G. Bn. S.L.I.(Pg)	HAUT HAMEAU		0950		
14 R.H.	BECLERS		1024		
D.Som.L.I.	HAVINNES		1041		
1 Section D.A.C.			—		

NOTE. Distance between units will be maintained as laid down in Provisional Standing Orders for the line of march.

Warning Order.

1. 229 Brigade group will be prepared to pass through the 231st Brigade tomorrow November 12th and hold outpost line on line S 25 central – II 19 central (approx)

2. 16th Devons will be on right.
   12th Somerset. L.I will be on the left.
   14th R.H will be in reserve

3. Battalions will establish posts under command of officers on all roads, railway, and canal crossings etc, along the outpost line.
   No civilians will be allowed to cross the line in either direction

4. Special parties will be detailed to ensure that junction is effected with flanks, Divisions. Points of junction between Battalion and flank Brigades to be reported

OC. 16 Devon
    12 SLI
    14 RH.
    229 TMB.
    117 Bde RFA.
    N°1 Sect DAC.   74th MGB.

Capt
Brigade Major
229th Inf Bde

SECRET   Copy No 14   WD

229 Infantry Brigade Order No 91.

Nov. 12th/18

Ref MAP.
Sheet 38 Scale 1/40,000.

1. In continuation of warning order issued, 229 Brigade group will march on 12th inst in accordance with attached table and take up the outpost line J.25.Central – D.19.Central. (Approximate.)

2. The Southern Boundary of the Division will be railway line between L'ANIQUE SAINT (I.26) and GHISLENGHIEN. (J.26)

3. Outpost sectors are allotted as follows:
   Right Sector. 16 DEVONS. RAILWAY in J.35b. incl and LA VERTE LOUCHE (excl)
   12th Som.L.I. between LA VERTE LOUCHE (incl) and D 19 Cent. (incl)

4. Brigade. H.Q. will close at LA HAMAIDE and open at WANNEBECQ at a time to be notified later.

5. If any opposition is encountered 229 Bde will halt when opposition is met with and establish outposts.

6. Completion of move to be reported immediately on arrival in new area.

7. All bridges across the DENDRE must be reconnoitred by advance parties.

8. Addressees to acknowledge.

Issued at 0200.

Addressed to.
     O.C. 16 DEVONS
     12. SOM.L.I.
     14. A.H.
     229. L.T.M.B.
     117 Bde R.F.A.
     74 M.G.B.
     No.1. Sect. R.A.F.

Copies to.
     A.P.C.
     Staff Captain
     Bde Sig Officer
     " 2nd "

J M Tuck.
Captain
Brigade Major
229. Inf Bde.

War Diary.
FILE.

MARCH TABLE.

to accompany Brigade Order No 91 Nov. 12/5/15.

Serial No	Unit	From	To	Route	Remarks
1.	1/Devons	LAHAMAIDE	STOQUOI Bn.H.Q	B.28, B.30, C.26. I.3, I.H. I.24.	
2.	12Som.L.I.	ESCALETTE	OLLIGNIES. Bn.H.Q	B.25, B.30, C.26. I.3, I.10.	
3.	14.R.H.	SARTIAU	ISIERES	B.25, B.30, I.2, I.8, I.15.	
4.	7u.M.G.Bn.	ROME.	GRAND MARAIS.	on for 14. R.H.	
5.	117.Bde.R.F.A.	DEUDE-GHIEN.	WANNEBECQ C.26	most direct route.	
6.	Bde.H.Q 225./T.M.B	CORNET.	WANNEBECQ C.26	most direct route.	
7.	No.1 Sect. D.A.C.	ROME	WANNEBECQ C.26	most direct route.	

Note. (a) Infantry will move off from their present billeting areas at 0900.
(b) Remainder of Units will move as soon as Infantry are clear of their billeting areas.
(c) Precedence on line of march will be in order shown above.

ADDENDA TO 229th INF. BDE. ORDER No. 92.   16-11-18.

1. The Staff Captain will meet Military (Billeting) parties as under :-

   229th M.G.Bn.   BRASSERIE. H.15.c.4.0. at 0900.

   229th L.T.M.B.)   Church MAINVAULT at 0930.
   12th Som. Regt.)

   Parties from other Units will proceed direct.

2. Precedence in line of march as shown in March Table.

3. Distances between Companies and Transport as laid down in F.S.R.

WD

SECRET.   Copy No. 17

229th BRIGADE ORDER NO. 92.

Map Ref. Sheet 57 & 38.   16th Nov. 1918.

1. The 229th Brigade Group will be relieved by the 87th Brigade Group, and 1 Company of 2nd Hants Regt. on 17th November and march West to an area as shown in attached table.

2. Details not mentioned in this order will be arranged between Commanding Officers concerned.

3. Halts for dinners will be made at discretion of Commanding Officers, during which halts, all troops and if possible vehicles will be kept clear of the road.

4. Completion of moves and march casualties to be reported forthwith to Bde. H.Q.

5. Brigade H.Q. will close at 1100 and open on arrival at MAINVAULT (H.31.b).

6. Addressees to acknowledge.

                                                        John Tuck
                                                        Captain,
                                                        Brigade Major,
                                                        229th Infantry Brigade.

Issued at ...1945...

By D.R.L.S. & runner.

Addressed to :-   Copies to :-

No. 1   O.C. 15th Devons.   R.G.C.
    2   "   12th Somerset L.I.   H.Q. 74th (Yeo) Div.
    3   "   14th Bl. Hrs.   "   87th Inf. Bde.
    4   "   229th L.T.M.B.   "   88th Inf. Bde.
    5   "   439 Fd. Coy. R.E.   Staff Captain.
    6   "   229th Fd. Ambulance.   Bde. Int. Officer.
    7   "   No. 1 Sect. D.A.C.   Bde. Sig. Officer.
    8   "   74th M.G. Bn.   War Diary.
    9   H.Q. 117th Bde. R.F.A.   File.

MARCH TABLE to accompany 229th Bde. Order No. 92. 16-11-18.

No.	Unit	Relieved by.	From.	To.	Route	Leave present area.	Remarks.
1.	229 Bde.H.Q.	87th B.H.Q.		H.31.b.		1000	Relieving Units not taking over Billets.
2.	229 L.T.M.B.	87th L.T.M.B.	WANNEBECQ.	MAINVAULT		0900	
3.	14th R.H.	1st Border Regt.	IZIERES.	MOUSTIER. L.29.c.cnt.(Sh.37)		0600	Personnel to be left behind to hand over Billets to 1st Border.
4.	16th Devons. (less outpost Coy.	1st K.O.S.B.	STOUQOI.	BUISSENAL G.20.cent.		On relief of outposts	Batts. will march out on arrival of relieving Units in Billeting area. Outposts will probably be relieved before arrival of those Units.
5.	Outpost Coy. 16th Devons.	2nd S.W.B.	OLLIGIES	MAINVAULT (H.31.b)	No Restriction	On relief of outposts.	
6.	12th Som.L.I. (less 3 northern posts).						
7.	3 Northern posts. 12th Som.L.I.	2nd Hants					
8.	439 Field Coy. R.E.	255 Field Coy. R.E.	FLORECQ.	REBAIX. I.19.c.		On arrival of 255Fd.Coy. in billeting area.	Pontoon Bridge at I.10.b.0.9. will be left in position until further orders.
9.	229 Field Ambulance.	37 Field Ambulance	OLLIGNIES	JOCQUEREAUMONT (P.5.a. Sh. 37)		0630	Personnel to be left behind to hand over billets to 87th Fd. Ambulance.
10.	117 Bde. R.F.A.			Cross roads 500 yds.N.W. of HACQUEGNIES		0800	On arrival at cross roads 500 yds.N.W. of HACQUEGNIES, 117 Bde. R.F.A. & No.1.Sect. D.A.C. will revert to control of C.R.A. & march to ANBAING-FOREST-POPULLIES-QUARTES area.
11.	No.1.Sect. D.A.C.			HACQUEGNIES L.27. (Sh. 37).			
12.	74th M.G.Bn.		GRAND-MARAIS.	RIGAULT. H.20.c.		0630	74th M.G.Bn. (less 2 Coys.) will stay night 17th/18th at RIGAULT, and proceed at 0900 on 18th to ELLIGNIES-LEZ-FRASNES-TEMOTE-PILE area and revert to Div. Control.

Ref. Sheets 30, 37 & 38.
Scale 1/40,000.

Headquarters, 229th Infantry Brigade.

Army Form C. 2118.

Instructions regarding War Diaries and Intelligence Summaries are contained in F.S. Regs., Part II. and the Staff Manual respectively. Title pages will be prepared in manuscript.

WAR DIARY
or
INTELLIGENCE SUMMARY.
(Erase heading not required.)

Place	Date	Hour	Summary of Events and Information	Remarks and references to Appendices
	1918. December.			
LEUZE.	1st to 3rd		Work continued on the Railway construction. (TOURNAI - BRUSSELS Main line) in the vicinity of the LEUZE - PIPAIX Sector.	
	5th		Brigadier General F.S. THACKERAY, D.S.O., M.C., returned from leave, and took over command of the Brigade from Lieut.-Col. G.S. POOLE, D.S.O., 12th Som. L.I.	
	7th		His Majesty the King reviewed the Division massed along the LEUZE - TOURNAI road in Square Q.34.	
	15th & 16th		229th Brigade Group moved to the GRAMMONT Area in accordance with Brigade Order No. 94 attached.	
			After the Brigade had been carefully billeted in the new area, the Educational Scheme was put on a good running basis. The attached pro-forma furnishes an idea of the number of students taking part and the nature of subjects being studied.	

C.J.G. Tuck.
Captain,
Brigade Major,
229th Infantry Brigade.

A.Q. 68.

229th Bde.
231st Bde.
"G"
A.D.M.S.

The attached sketch shews the boundary between the 229th Inf. Bde. Group and the 231st Inf. Bde. Group in GRAMMONT. The 231st Field Ambulance will be accommodated in OLIGNIES. The 231st Inf. Bde will allot a suitable building or buildings in their part of GRAMMONT for the 229th Field Ambulance and advise this Office as soon as they have done so.

In allotting billets Halls and theatres will not be used for accommodating men without reference to this Office. These are required as Recreation Rooms and Concert and Lecture Halls.

Each Brigade will as soon as possible send to this Office a complete list of the Halls and Theatres in their respective areas giving dimensions.

H. Burchart

Major,

D.A.A.G. 74th (Yeomanry) Division.

2/12/18.

No. Sketch to A.D.M.S.

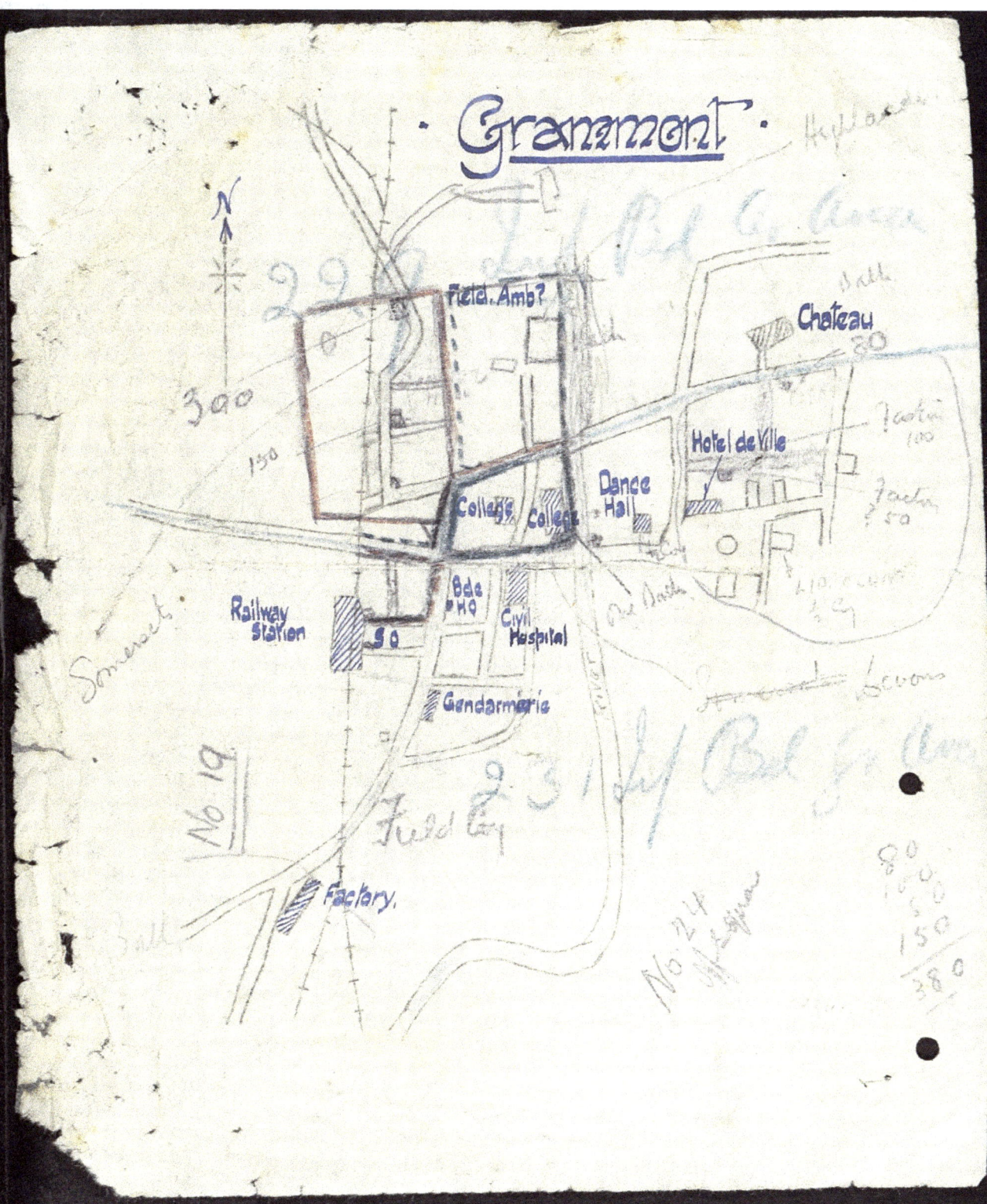

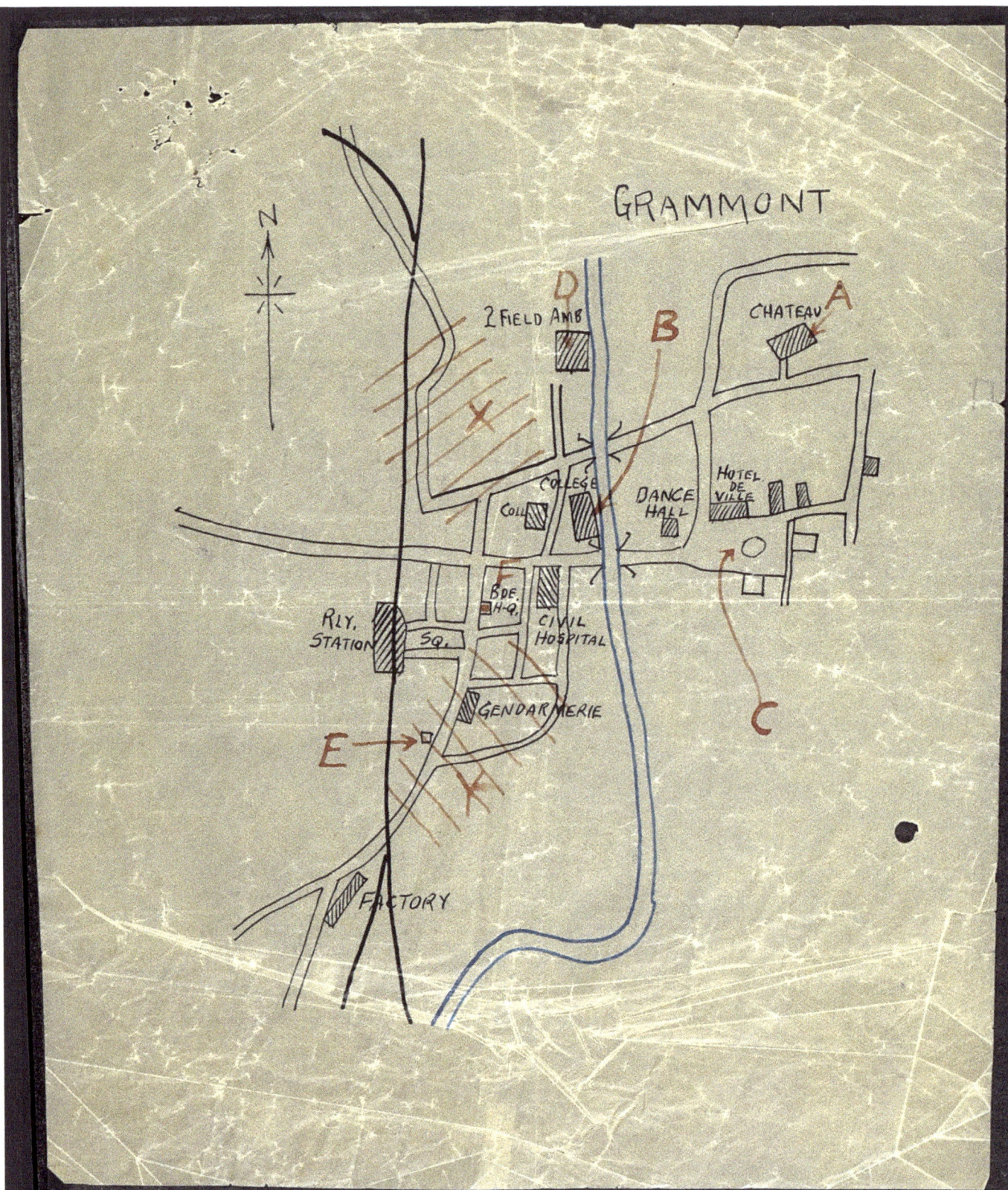

INSTRUCTIONS FOR ADVANCED BILLETING PARTIES
REFERENCE 74th DIV. WARNING ORDER dated 6th December 1918.

1. Advanced Billeting parties will move to the New Area on 11th inst, by Motor Lorries as under :-

2. Composition of Party.

	Offrs.	O.Rs.	Bicycles.
Each Inf. Bde. H.Q. & C.R.A.			
Staff Captain.			
Interpreter.			
1 Other Rank.			
Total for 3 Inf.Bdes. & C.R.A.	4	8	4
Each Inf.Battn. (incldg Pioneers & M.G.Battn.)			
1 Officer.			
4 O.Q.M.S.			
1 Representative Bn.H.Q.			
Total for 11 Battalions.	11	55	-
Each Fd.Coy. R.E., F.Ambce. & Div. Signals.			
1 Off. & 1 Sergt.			
3 Field Coys. R.E.	3	3	
3 Field Ambulances.	3	3	
Div.Sig.Coy.	1	1	
74th Divisional Train.			
4 Officers & 4 N.C.Os.	4	4	
Each Field Art.Bde and the D.A.C.			
Adjutant.	4		
Each Battery & Section D.A.C. & Bde.A.C.			
1 Officer & 1 B.Q.M.S.	13	13	
TOTALS	43	87	4

3. A Bicycle will be taken for each Staff Captain proceeding.

4. Lorries will report as under :-

	No of Lorries Allotted.	Place at which lorries will report.	Hour at which lorry will report.
229th Inf.Bde.Group plus 1 & 2 Coys Div. Train less Fld Ambce *PIONEER Bᵗ*	2	229th Inf.Bde. H.Q. LEUZE.	0900
230th Inf.Bde.Group less Fld Ambce.	2	Cross Roads. Q.35.c.6.4. LAMBART.	0900
231st Inf.Bde.Group plus Nos 3 & 4 Coys. Train less Fld.Ambce. *MG Bᵗ*	2	Cross Roads. K.27.c.3.0. QUARTES.	0900
Div.Arty. Group.	2	Cross Roads. L.25.a.3.0. DIME.	0900

5. Rations for 96 hours will be carried by each Officer and other rank.

6. Brigadier Generals will issue the necessary orders to the Field Coys affiliated to their Groups and to the Bde / Train Coys whose parties are proceeding under their orders. One of the 229th Inf.Bde. Group lorries will collect all the advanced Parties of the Train at GRAMMONT and take them to VIANE.
   The Advanced Parties of the Field Ambulances & Signal Coy will be sent forward under arrangements to be made by the A.D.M.S. and O.C. Div.Signal Coy respectively.

7. All lorries will proceed via ATH.

8. Acknowledge.

(signed) Jourens
Lieut.Col.

7th December 1918.   A.A.&Q.M.G., 74th (Yeomanry) Division.

Copies to :-
- Headquarters.
- 229th Inf.Bde.   A.D.M.S.   War Diary
- 230th Inf.Bde.   Train.   VI. Corps Q
- 231st Inf.Bde.   O.C. Signals.
- C.R.A.   "G.S."
- C.R.E.   File

INSTRUCTIONS FOR ADVANCED BILLETING PARTIES
REFERENCE 74th DIV. WARNING ORDER dated 6th December 1918.

1. Advanced Billeting parties will move to the New Area on 11th inst. by Motor Lorries as under :-

2. <u>Composition of Party.</u>

	Offrs.	O.Rs.	Bicycles.
<u>Each Inf. Bde. H.Q. & O.R.A.</u>			
Staff Captain.			
Interpreter.			
1 Other Rank.			
Total for 3 Inf. Bdes. & O.R.A.	4	8	4
<u>Each Inf. Battn.</u> (incldg Pioneers & M.G.Battn.)			
1 Officer.			
4 O.& M.S.			
1 Representative Bn.H.Q.			
Total for 11 Battalions.	11	55	-
<u>Each Fd. Coy. R.E., F.Amb. & Div. Signals.</u>			
1 Off. & 1 Sergt.			
3 Field Coys. R.E.	3	3	
3 Field Ambulances.	3	3	
Div. Sig. Coy.	1	1	
<u>74th Divisional Train.</u>			
4 Officers & 4 R.C.Coy.	4	4	
<u>Each Field Art.Bde and the D.A.C.</u>			
Adjutant.	4		
<u>Each Battery & Section D.A.C. & Bde.A.C.</u>			
1 Officer & 1 B.Q.M.S.	13	13	
TOTALS	43	87	4

3. A Bicycle will be taken for each Staff Captain proceeding.

4. Lorries will report as under :-

	No of Lorries Allotted.	Place at which lorries will report.	Hour at which lorry will report.
229th Inf.Bde.Group plus 1 & 2 Coys Div. Train less Fld Amblce PIONEERS	2	229th Inf.Bde. H.Q. LEUZE.	0300
230th Inf.Bde.Group less Fld.Amblce.	2	Cross Roads. Q.35.c.5.4. LADEUZE.	0300
231st Inf.Bde.Group plus Nos 3 & 4 Coys. Train less Fld.Amblce. MG Bn	2	Cross Roads K.27.c.3.0. QUARTES.	0300
Div.Arty. Group.	2	Cross Roads. L.25.a.5.0. DIXE.	0300.

5. Rations for 96 hours will be carried by each Officer and other rank.

6. Brigadier Generals will issue the necessary orders to the Field Coys affiliated to their Groups and to the Bde Train Coys whose parties are proceeding under their orders. One of the 229th Inf.Bde. Group lorries will collect all the advanced Parties of the Train at GRAMONT and take them to VIANE.
    The Advanced Parties of the Field Ambulances & Signal Coy will be sent forward under arrangements to be made by the A.D.M.S. and O.C. Div.Signal Coy respectively.

7. All lorries will proceed via ATH.

8. Acknowledge.

[signature]

[signature] Lieut.Col.

7th December 1918. A.A.&Q.M.G., 74th (Yeomanry) Division.

Copies to :-
　　Headquarters.
　　229th Inf.Bde.　　A.D.M.S.　　War Diary
　　230th Inf.Bde.　　Train.　　　II Corps Q
　　231st Inf.Bde.　　O.C. Signals.　M.G.B.
　　C.R.A.　　　　　　"G.S."
　　C.R.E.　　　　　　File.

INSTRUCTIONS FOR ADVANCED BILLETING PARTIES.
REFERENCE 74TH DIV. WARNING ORDER dated 6th December 1915.

1. Advanced Billeting parties will move to the New Area on 11th inst. by Motor Lorries as under :-

2. **Composition of Party.**

	Offrs.	O.Rs.	Bicycles.
Each Inf. Bde. H.Q. & C.R.A.			
Staff Captain.			
Interpreter.			
1 Other Rank.			
Total for 3 Inf. Bdes. & C.R.A.	4	8	4
Each Inf. Battn. (incldg Pioneers & M.G.Battn.)			
1 Officer.			
4 C.Q.M.S.			
1 Representative Bn.H.Q.			
Total for 11 Battalions.	11	55	-
Each Fd.Coy. R.E., F.Amblce. & Div. Signals.			
1 Off. & 1 Sergt.			
3 Field Coys. R.E.	3	3	
3 Field Ambulances.	3	3	
Div. Sig. Coy.	1	1	
74th Divisional Train.			
4 Officers & 4 N.C.Os.	4	4	
Each Field Art. Bde and the D.A.C.			
Adjutant.	4		
Each Battery & Section D.A.C. & Bde.A.C.			
1 Officer & 1 B.Q.M.S.	13	13	
TOTALS	43	87	4

3. A Bicycle will be taken for each Staff Captain proceeding.

4. Lorries will report as under :-

	No of Lorries Allotted.	Place at which lorries will report.	Hour at which lorry will report.
229th Inf.Bde.Group plus 1 & 2 Coys Div. Train less Fld Amblce *Pioneer Bn*	2	229th Inf.Bde. H.Q. LEUZE.	0900
230th Inf.Bde.Group less Fld Amblce.	2	Cross Roads. Q.35.c.6.4. MARBAIX.	0900
231st Inf.Bde.Group plus Nos 3 & 4 Coys. Train less Fld.Amblce.	2	Cross Roads. K.27.c.3.0. QUARRIES.	0900
Div.Arty. Group.	2	Cross Roads. L.33.a.3.0. DIME.	0900

5. Rations for 96 hours will be carried by each Officer and other rank.

6. Brigadier Generals will issue the necessary orders to the Field Coys affiliated to their Groups and to the Train Coys whose parties are proceeding under their orders. One of the 229th Inf.Bde. Group lorries will collect all the advanced Parties of the Train at GRAMONT and take them to VIANE.
   The Advanced Parties of the Field Ambulances & Signal Coy will be sent forward under arrangements to be made by the A.D.M.S. and O.C. Div.Signal Coy respectively.

7. All lorries will proceed via ATH.

8. Acknowledge.

                                       Couzens
                                                          Lieut.Col.
7th December 1918.   A.A.&Q.M.G., 74th (Yeomanry) Division.

Copies to :-
    Headquarters.
    229th Inf.Bde.   A.D.M.S.
    230th Inf.Bde.   Train.
    231st Inf.Bde.   O.C. Signals.
    C.R.A.   "G.S."
    C.R.E.

HEADQUARTERS
229th INFANTRY BDE.
Date 6/12/18
Ref. No. 38

SECRET.   G.S. 155.

WARNING ORDER.

1.   The move to the new area will probably begin about December 13th.

2.   Billetting parties will be sent forward two days in advance of the troops under instructions to be issued by 74th Division 'A'.

                                        [signature]
                                        for Lieut-Colonel,
                                        General Staff,
                                        74th (Yeomanry) Division.

6th December 1918.

                Copies to:-
                        G.O.C.
                        'G'.
                        'Q'.
                        C.R.A.
                        C.R.E.
                        Signal Company.
                        Machine Gun Battn.
                        229th Inf. Bde.
                        230th Inf. Bde.
                        231st Inf. Bde.
                        A.D.M.S.
                        Div. Train.
                        D.A.D.V.S.
                        D.A.P.M.
                        Camp Commandant.

SECRET.

ADMINISTRATIVE INSTRUCTIONS

reference move of 229th Infantry Bde. to GRAMMONT AREA.

1. The move of 74th Division to New Area will commence about 13th December.

2. Advanced Billeting Parties will proceed to New Area on 11th instant by motor lorries.

3. In addition to parties from units of 229th Infantry Brigade, parties from the following units will also proceed under orders of B.G.C., 229th Infantry Brigade :-

    439th Field Coy. R.E.
    12th Bn. Loyal North Lancs Regt. (Pioneers)
    Nos. 1 and 2 Coys. Divisional Train.

4. Billeting parties will be composed as under :-

    Each Bn. (incld.
      Pioneer Bn.)   1 Officer, 4 C.Q.M.S. & representat-
                                         -ives from Bn. Hqrs.
    229th L.T.M.B.   1 Officer.
    439 Fd.Coy.R.E.   1 Officer and 1 Sergt.
    Each Train Coy.   1 Officer and 1 N.C.O.

5. Parties will report to Staff Captain at Bde. Hqrs, 60 RUE CONDE, LEUZE, at 0745 on the 11th inst. With the exception of the party from 439 Field Coy. which will join lorries at road junction N.13.c.2.2. (sheet 36) at 0815.

6. Rations for 96 hours will be carried by each officer and other rank. Bicycles will not be taken.

7. On arrival at GRAMMONT one lorry will collect all the advance parties from the Divisional Train at the STATION and take them to VINNE.

8. Addressees to acknowledge.

7-12-18.

Captain,
Staff Captain,
229th Infantry Brigade.

Addressed to :-
No. 1. O.C. 16th Devons.
   2.   "   12th Som. L.I.
   3.   "   14th Royal Hqrs.
   4.   "   229th L.T.M.B.
   5.   "   439 Fd. Coy.R.E.
   6.   "   12th Bn. L.N.L.(P).
   7.   "   No.1 Coy.Div.Train.
   8.   "   No.2 "   "   "
   9.   "   Div. Train.

Copies to :-

B.G.C.
B.M.
O.C.Sigs.
O.C. Bde. Hqrs.

HEADQUARTERS
229th ...
Date 10/12/18
Ref. No. 38

O.C. 16th Devons.
12th Somerset L.I.
439 Fd. Coy. R.E.

      The following wire received from 74th Division is forwarded for information :-

    " Warning order. Move to new area commences
    " tomorrow. Details later. "

                                        Captain,
                                    Brigade Major,
10-12-18.   229th Infantry Brigade.

To:- Headquarters,
      229th. Brigade.

    I beg to acknowledge receipt of **ADMINISTRATIVE INSTRUCTIONS** reference Move; dated 7/12/18.
    Confirming telephone conversation with the Staff Captain this afternoon, this Battalion will be billetted in **LESSINES**. Instructions for same have been received through the O.R.E. and the billetting of all ranks has already been completed in that town. It will therefore not be necessary for the billetting party to be sent with the Brigade.

8/12/18.

O. Commanding,
1/12th. Loyal North Lancashire Regt. (Pnrs.)

O.C., 16th Devon Regt.
O.C., 12th Som.L.I.
O.C., 439th Fld.Coy. R.E.

Reference my 38 Warning Order of today :-

The move of the Brigade is postponed for four days.

Captain,
Brigade Major,
229th Infantry Brigade.

10-12-18.

3 Bns.
LTMB
439 Fd Coy.

Copy No...... 10

SECRET.

74th DIVISION ORDER No.118.

10th December 1918.

Ref.Maps. TOURNAI & BRUSSELS Sheets.
1:100,000.

1. On X, Y and Z days the Division will march to the area LESSINES - GRAMMONT - HERINNES.

2. The move will be carried out in accordance with the attached March Table.

3. The Division will march with intervals as laid down in F.S.Reg. Part I, page 50.

4. Administrative Instructions relative to the move will be issued by the A.A. & Q.M.G.

5. Divisional Headquarters will close at FRASNES lez BUISSENAL at 1200 hours on 'X' day and open at LESSINES at the same hour.

6. ACKNOWLEDGE.

C Broad

Lieut.Colonel,
General Staff,
74th (Yeomanry) Division.

Issued at...... 1800

Copies to:-
No.1. G.O.C.
    2. 'G'
  3-5. 'Q'
    6. C.R.A.
    7. C.R.E.
    8. Signal Company.
    9. M.G.Battn.
  10. 229th Inf.Bde.
  11. 230th " "
  12. 231st " "
  13. A.D.M.S.
  14. Div.Train.

No.15. D.A.D.V.S.
  16. D.A.P.M.
  17. Camp Commandant.
18-19. III Corps.
  20. 8th Division.
  21. 15th Division.
  22. 55th Division.
  23. H.A., III Corps.
24-25. War Diary.
  26. File.

S E C R E T.

MARCH TABLE. (To accompany 74th (Yeo) Division Order No 118).

1. Serial No.	2. Date.	3. Unit.	4. From	5. To	6. Route.	7. Remarks.
1	X	242 Bde R.F.A.	MONCEAU	R.A. area excluding GHOY and LES DEUX ACREN.	via main FRASNES lez BUISSENAL – LESSINES rd.	To be clear of FRASNES lez BUISSENAL by 1100.
2		Pioneer Bn.	FRASNES	LESSINES.	as above	Starting point X roads FRASNES at 1115.
3		Div. H.Q.	"	"	"	" " " " FRASNES at 1125.
4		74th Bn M.G.C.	"	"	"	" " " " FRASNES at 1130.
5		229 Bde Group.	LEUZE – MOUSTIER area.	LA HAMAIDE – OSTICHES – OEUDEGHIEN.	GD METZ – HOUTAING – MONTAGNE.	14th R.H. via FRASNES and main road to LA HAMAIDE not to enter FRASNES before 1115.
6		230 Bde Group.	BARRY – MAISART – THIMOUGIES.	FRASNES lez BUISSENAL – BUISSENAL.	no restrictions as to route except that TOURNAI – LEUZE road may not be used.	To be clear of X roads at HACQUEGNIES and BAS DOUX by 1400. 230th Field Ambce to join 230 Bde Group on arrival at FRASNES.
7		231 Bde Group	LA TOMBE – VELAINES – RAVINES.	MONTROEUL au BOIS – HERQUEG LES – MOUSTIER.	no restrictions.	Not to enter new area (Col.5) before 1200.
8	Y	229 Bde Group.	LA HAMAIDE – OSTICHES – OEUDEGHIEN.	GRAMMONT area.	LESSINES.	Billets to be clear by 1000.
9		230 Bde Group.	FRASNES area	LES deux ACREN – OGY – REMANPONT – GHOY – SCAUBECQ area.	LA HAMAIDE.	To be clear of FRASNES by 1000.
10		231 Bde Group.	MONTROEUL au BOIS MOUSTIER area.	LA HAMAIDE – OSTICHES – OEUDEGHIEN.	FRASNES.	Not to enter FRASNES before 1000.

- 2 -

1 Serial No.	2 Date.	3 Unit.	4 From	5 TO	6 ROUTE	7 REMARKS.
11	Z	230 Bde Group.	LES DEUX ACREN area.	BIEVENE - HERINNES area.	no restrictions	To be east of LESSINES - GRAMONT rd by 1030.
12	Z	231 Bde Group.	LA HAMAIDE area.	GRAMONT area.	LESSINES.	Not to enter LESSINES before 1030. 231 Fld Ambce leaves 231 Bde Group at LESSINES coming under orders of A.D.M.S.
13	Z	Div.Arty less 242 Bde AFA.	CORDES - FOREST area.	LES DEUX ACREN VIANE area.	FRASNES - LESSINES.	

S E C R E T.
* * * * *

S.G. 157.

13th December, 1918.

Reference Divisional Order No 118.

1. 'X' day will be December 15th.
2. ACKNOWLEDGE.

[signature]

Lieut-Colonel,
General Staff,
74th (Yeomanry) Division.

Issued at 1000.

Distribution as for Divisional Order No 118.

SECRET.

HEADQUARTERS
229th INFANTRY BDE.
Date ...
Ref. No. 59

C.Q.601/4.

Headquarters.
229th Inf.Bde.   C.R.A.
230th Inf.Bde.   C.R.E. (for 1/12th L.N.Lancs.)
231st Inf.Bde.   O.C. 74th M.G.Battn.

      Reference this Office C.Q.601/3 of 12th instant, para 2.

1.   The following Formations and Units will send guides to these Headquarters, FRASNES LES BUISSENAL at 0800 on the 15th instant to take over the lorries allotted to them.-

      229th Inf.Bde.
      230th Inf.Bde.
      231st Inf.Bde.
      242nd A.F.A.Bde.
      1/12th L.N.Lancs (Pioneers).
      74th M.G.Battn.
      74th Div. Train.

2.   The 229th Inf.Bde, 242 A.F.A.Bde, L.N.Lancs, and 74th.M.G.Battn will ensure that their lorries are returned to Divisional Headquarters at LESSINES immediately after arrival at the respective destinations. This includes any lorries at present with Units for the purchase of Xmas Stores.

3.   The C.R.A. will detail guides to report at the Church FRASNES at 0800 on the 17th instant to take over the 8 lorries allotted to the Div.Arty.Bdes on that day.

4.   ACKNOWLEDGE.

                                                Major.
                                               D.A.Q.M.G.,
13th December 1918.   74th (Yeo) Division.

SECRET.   Copy No. 1....

ADMINISTRATIVE INSTRUCTIONS RELATIVE TO   C.Q.601/3
74th DIVISION ORDER No.118.

Ref.Maps. TOURNAI & BRUSSELS Sheets. 1/100,000.   12th December 1918.

1. SHELTERS. Immediately on arrival in the new area, Units will indent on the Field Coys. R.E. for material to make Shelters for Cooks, Guards, Stable Picquets, Sentries etc, where there are none provided by existing buildings.
O.C. 74th Divisional Train will communicate direct with the C.R.E. regarding shelters etc. at the Refilling Points.

2. TRANSPORT. O.C. 74th Divisional Train will arrange to hand over Baggage & Supply Wagons on X-1 day.
The Baggage Wagons will be returned to the Divisional Train on the day following the arrival in the new area. The Supply Wagons will be retained until further orders.
The C.R.A. will arrange to Horse 12 Baggage Wagons of the Divisional Train. These Baggage Wagons accompanying the Artillery on the march.
The following additional Transport will be provided. The Horse Transport will be issued to the Divisional Train on X-1 day under instructions to be issued later and O.C. Divisional Train will arrange for the distribution to Units and ultimate collection. The Motor Lorries will report on the first day of the move of Formations or Units and will be returned immediately after arrival at destinations. Units staging for one or more nights en route will thus retain their lorries until they reach their final destinations.

UNIT.	LORRIES.	G.S.WAGONS complete with teams & Drivers.
229th Infantry Bde.	5	4
230th Infantry Bde.	5	4
231st Infantry Bde.	5	4
242 A.F.A. Brigade.	4	-
L.N.Lancs. (Pioneers)	1	2
74th M.G. Battalion.	1	2
74th Div. Train (For supplies)	1	-
74th Div. Artillery.	8	-

The above are exclusive of Lorries purchasing Xmas Stores, which can be retained when they return and used for purposes of the move.

3. SUPPLIES. The following table shows the times and places for refilling. These are subject to alteration as soon as Railhead moves forward :-

X DAY.

UNIT.	REFILLING POINT.	TIME.	REMARKS.
229th Inf.Bde.Group.	FRASNES LEZ BUISSENAL.	0800	
230th Inf.Bde.Group.	-do-	1400	
231 Inf.Bde.Group.	-do-	1500	
Divnl.Headquarters) 74th Div.Signals.) 1/12th L.N.Lancs.) 74th M.G.Battn.) 242 A.F.A.Brigade.)	-do-	0900	
74th Div.Arty.	QUARTES.	0900	

-2-

Y DAY.

UNIT.	REFILLING POINT.	TIME.	REMARKS.
229th Inf.Bde.Group.	GRAMMONT.	1500	
230 Inf.Bde.Group.	FRASNES LEZ BUISSENAL.	0800	
231 Bde. Group.	-do-	0900	
Div.Headquarters.			Until
Div. Signals.			further
1/12 L.H.Lancs.	LESSINES.	0900	notice.
74th M.G.Battn.			
242 Brigade R.F.A			
74 Div.Arty.	QUARTES.	0900	

Z DAY.

229th Inf.Bde.Group	GRAMMONT.	0900	(Until further (notice.
230th Inf.Bde.Group.	VIANE.	1400	
231 Inf.Bde.Group.	GRAMMONT.	1400	
74th Div.Arty.	LESSINES.	1500	

Z plus 1 DAY.

230th Inf.Bde.Group.	VIANE.	0900	(Until
231st Inf.Bde.Group.	GRAMMONT.	1000	(further
74th Div.Arty.	LESSINES.	1000	(notice.

4. DIVISIONAL TRAIN. The Train Companies will move to the new area under orders to be issued by the O.C.Train.

5. ACKNOWLEDGE.

[signature]

[signature] Lieut.Colonel.
A.A. & Q.M.G.
74th (Yeo) Division.

Copies to :- No.1. 229th Inf.Bde. 11 Camp Commandant.
2. 230th Inf.Bde. 12 74th M.G.Battalion.
3. 231st Inf.Bde. 13. 74 Signal Coy.
4-5 C.R.A. 14. 74 Div. Train.
6-7 C.R.E. 15 "G"
8 A.D.M.S. 16 74th M.T.Company.
9. D.A.D.V.S. 17. War Diary.
10. D.A.D.O.S. 18-19 Spare.

Administrative Instruction Issued
in connection with Bde. Order No.

1. Shelters.
Immediately on arrival in new area units will submit indent to the Office for material to make shelters for Cooks, guards, stable picquet, sentries &c where there are none provided by existing buildings.

2. Transport.
Baggage and supply wagons will report to Units today 14th inst. day - the former will be returned to the Train on the day following the arrival in the new area, the latter will be retained until further orders.
The following additional transport will be provided. The lorries will report on the 5 units at a time to be notified later per day of the move & will be retained until the final destination is reached when they will be immediately returned to Division. Extra horse transport will report on X-1 day & will be retained pending further instruction.

	Lorries.	G.S. wagons complete with horses & drivers.
Each Bn.	2	1
Field Coy	1	—
Bde Hqr & LTMB.		

3. Repelling Point.
X day	FRASNES LEZ BUISSENAL	at 0800.
Y day	GRAMMONT	at 1500
Z day	Do.	at 0900

and until further orders

4. Transport Lines.
Location of transport lines to be notified to the Office immediately on arrival.

— over —

(5) Halls & Theatres.

These will not be used as billets as same are required as Recreation Rooms, & concert & lecture Halls.

Units will forward as soon as possible a list of Halls & Theatres in their respective areas giving location and dimensions.

(6) Billeting Parties.

Billeting parties to report to Staff Capt. at 1000 hours on X day at X roads. B 25d 3.7 (Sheet 38)

Could ладd letter meet these parties as well in case I can get back there.

No. CO575

ADMINISTRATIVE INSTRUCTIONS RELATIVE TO
74th DIVISIONAL ORDER No. 116.

TRAFFIC ORDERS FOR MOVES OF M.T.

Reference 1/100,000 Map.   15th December 1918.

1. On 15th December 1918.

    (a) Lorries of Divnl.H.Q., H.Q. R.A., 242 Army Bde. R.F.A., M.G.Bn and Pioneer Battalion will proceed via ELLEZELLES to LESSINES to be clear of FRASNES by 0930.

    (b) 229th Inf. Bde. Lorries will proceed via FRASNES - LAHAMAIDE Road and will not enter FRASNES before 1145 hours. These lorries will not pass or attempt to pass any troops on the road moving from WEST to EAST.

    (c) 230th Inf. Bde. Lorries via BARRY MAULD and LEUZE to FRASNES and will not pass LEUZE before 1200 hours.

    (d) 231st Inf. Bde. Lorries via TOURNAI-LEUZE-HACQUEGNIES Road, not to pass LEUZE before 1400.

2. On 16th December 1918.

    (a) 229th Inf. Bde. Lorries via LESSINES to GRAMMONT and return by same road to LESSINES, not to leave GRAMMONT on return journey before 1400.

    (b) 230th Inf. Bde. Lorries via ELLEZELLES and LESSINES to be clear of FRASNES by 1000 and LESSINES 1400.

    (c) 231st Inf. Bde. Lorries via FRASNES - LAHAMAIDE Road not to pass FRASNES before 1000.

    (d) Lorries being returned from LESSINES to FRASNES will proceed via ELLEZELLES and will not leave LESSINES before 1400.

3. On 17th December 1918.

    (a) 230th Inf. Bde. Lorries via LESSINES - GRAMMONT Road via GRAMMONT & VIANE. To be clear of GRAMMONT by 1100.

    (b) 231st Inf. Bde. Lorries via LESSINES not to enter LESSINES before 1030.

    (c) Divisional Artillery Lorries via ELLEZELLES and to be clear of FRASNES before Brigades and D.A.C. enter.

[signature]
Lieut.Col.
A.A.& Q.M.G., 74th (Yeo) Division.

Issued at

Copies to :-
1. "G"
2-5. "A & Q"
6. C.R.A.
7. C.R.E.
8. O.C. Signals.
9. M.G.Battalion.
10. 229 Inf Bde f HA
11. 230 "
12. 231 "
13. RAMC

14. O.C.Div.Train.
15. D.A.D.V.S.
16-17. D.A.P.M.
18. Camp Commandant.
19-20. War Diary.
21-22. File.

W.D.

SECRET.   Copy No.........

229th BRIGADE ORDER No. 94

Ref.Map Sheets 37, 38 and 39.   13th December 1918.
   Scale 1:40,000.

1. On the 15th and 16th December the Brigade will march to the GRAMMONT Area in accordance with attached Table.

2. Brigade Headquarters will close at 1100 on December 15th at LEUZE and reopen at the same hour at CORNET (LA HAMAIDE) and will close at 1100 on December 16th at CORNET and reopen at the same hour at the Chateau ½ mile N.of the O in GRAMMONT.

3. Further Administrative Orders will be issued separately.

4. Addressees to Acknowledge.

                                                    A.M. Tuck
                                                    Captain,
                                                    Brigade Major,
                                                    229th Infantry Brigade.

Issued at 1600
by D.R.L.S. & Runner.

Addressed to :-   Copies to :-

   No.1 16th Devons   No.8 B.G.C., 229th Infy.Bde.
      2 12th Som.L.I.   9 Staff Captain,
      3 14th Bl.Highlrs.   10 Brigade Signalling Officer
      4 229th L.T.M.B.   11   "   Intelligence   "
      5 439th Fld.Coy.R.E.   12 74th (Yeo) Division.
      6 229th Field Amb.   13 Town Major, LEUZE.
      7 448th Coy. A.S.C.

MARCH TABLE issued with 229th Brigade Order No.94.

Serial No.	Date.	Unit.	From.	To.	Starting Point.	Pass Starting Point.	Remarks.
1	Dec. 15th	439th Fld. Coy.R.E.	HOUTAING	OSTICHES			To be clear of HOUTAING by 1000. Via FRASNES. To enter FRASNES by 1115, but not before.
2		14th R.H.	MOUSTIER	LA HAMAIDE.			Route :- GRAND METZ - HOUTAING - MONTAGNE.
3		12th Som. L.I.	LUZE	OSTICHES	R.24.a.3.4.	0830	
4		16th Devon Regt.	PIPAIX	OUDEGHIEN.	"	0838	do
5		229th Fld. Amb.	LEUZE	OUDEGHIEN	"	0846	do
6		229th L.T. M.B.	LEUZE	LA HAMAIDE	"	0901	do
7	Dec. 16th	439th Fld. Coy.R.E.	OSTICHES	GRAMMONT	Road Junction at B.30.b.95.80	1000	
8		12th Som. L.I.	OSTICHES	"	"	1005	
9		14th R.H.	LA HAMAIDE	"	"	1013	LESSINES the direct route.
10		16th Devon Regt.	OUDEGHIEN	"	"	1021	
11		229th Field Amb.	OUDEGHIEN	"	"	1029	
12		229th L.T.M.B.	LA HAMAIDE.	"	"	1034	

NOTE :-
1. Intervals as laid down in F.S.R. PartI, page 50.
2. Halts of 10 minutes as 10 minutes to the clock hour will be observed.
3. Halts from 1150 to 1300 for dinners will be made.

ADMINISTRATIVE INSTRUCTIONS

issued in connection with Brigade Order No. 94.

December 15th, 1918.

1. **Shelters.** Immediately on arrival in the new area, Units will indent *through Bde H.Q.* on the Field Coys, R.E. for material to make Shelters for Cooks, Guards, Stable Picquets, Sentries, etc, where there are none provided by existing buildings.

2. **Baggage and Supply Wagons.** These will report to Units to-day 14th Instant. The former will be returned to the train on the day following arrival in the new area. The latter will be retained until further orders.

3. **Lorries.**
    (a) The following additional transport will be provided. Units (less 14 R.H.) as shown below will send guides to Bde.H.Q. to report to the Staff Captain, at 0830 on 15th instant, who will guide lorries to their respective H.Qrs.

	Lorries.	G.S. Wagons complete with team & driver.
Each Bn.	2	1
Field Coy. R.E.	-	1
Bde. H.Q. & L.T.M.B.	1	-

    (b) 2 Lorries *for* 14 R.H. will be handed over at MOUSTIER by Brigade representative *(in para 3(a))*. Lorries shown above include the two lorries at present purchasing Xmas stores, which on return will be re-allotted.

    (c) 22 Inf. Bde. lorries on the 15th instant will proceed via FRASNES - LAHAMAIDE Road and will not enter FRASNES before 1145 hours. These lorries will not pass or attempt to pass any troops on the road moving from WEST to EAST.

    (d) 22 Brigade lorries on the *16th* inst will be returned to Divisional H.Q. at LESSINES not earlier than 1400 or later than 1500. *leaving GRAMMONT*.

4. **Refilling Point.**

    | December 15th. | FRASNES LES BUISSENAL | at | 0800. |
    | 16th. | GRAMMONT | at | 1500. |
    | 17th. | " | at | 0900. |

    and until further notice.

5. **Transport Lines.**

    Location of transport lines will be notified to this office immediately on arrival.

(over)

6. **Halls & Theatres.**

These will not be used as billets as same are required as recreation rooms, concert halls and Lecture Rooms. Units will forward as soon as possible list of Halls and Theatres in their respective area giving location and dimensions.

7. **Football grounds.**

No football grounds will be reserved by Units. These will be allotted by the Brigade Sports Committee.

8. **Billeting Parties.**

Billeting parties for move to LAHAMAIDE area will report to the Staff Captain at 1000 on 15th inst at cross roads at B.25.d.3.7 (sheet 28).

9. Addressees to acknowledge.

a.f.M.Tuck.
Captain,
Brigade Major,
229th Infantry Brigade.

Addressed to :-

16th Devons.
12th Som. L.I.
14th Royal H-drs.
229th L.T.M.B.
439th Fld. Coy. R.E.
229th Fd. Amb.
448th Coy. A.S.C.

Copies to :-

B.G.C. 229th Inf. Bde.
Staff Captain.
Brigade Signalling Officer.
       "   Intelligence   "
74th (Y&) Division.
Town Major, LUZE.

EDUCATION GROUP No.3 (229th Inf. Bde.)
GENERAL CLASSIFICATION.

Unit.	16th Devons.	12th S.L.I.	14th R.H.	229th L.T.M.B.	229th F.A.	443th A.S.C.	439th R.E.	Bde. H.Q.	Total.
No. of N.C.O's and Men.	920	600	780	52	191	77	191	81	2892
No. requiring instruction.	606	265	506	37	90	12	170	57	1743
No. who have reached Matric. standard.	-	-	64	-	30	-	-	5	99
No. requiring:- Course A.	312	60	73	6	-	3	62	8	524
Course B.	112	57	232	22	50	8	20	13	514
Course C.	159	70	139	4	40	1	88	17	518

COURSES D - J.

Unit.	16th Devons.	12th S.L.I.	14th R.H.	229th L.T.M.B.	229th F.Amb.	448th A.S.C.	439th R.E.	Bde. H.Q.	Total.	Lecturers.	Instructors.
No. requiring:- 1. Comm.Geog. 'D'		1			2				3	Pte. THOMPSON, W.H. Lt. DICKSON.	Lt. ARNOTT, 14th R.H. Lt. CROOKSHANK, R.E. C.S.M. HURLEY, R.E. Pte. HOWIE,
2. French	35	23	57	1	11	4	14	22	167		Pte. BARRETT, S.L.I. Lt. ARNOTT, R.H. 2/Lt. GOURLAY, "
3. Italian.	2								2		
4. German			4		2		1		7		2/Lt. BROWN, R.H.
5. Spanish.			1		2		1	1	5		
6. Shorthand.	14	19	49	4	6		4	8	104		L/C. PARSONS, Devons 2/Lt. RICHARDS, S.L.I. Lt. ARNOTT, R.H. 2/Lt. GOURLAY, do Cpl. WALKER, R.E.
7. Book-keeping.	34	15	66	6	7	1	8	18	155		Pte. JUDGE, S.L.I. Sgt. HANNAH, Cpl. WALKER, R.E.
8. Typewriting.	2	1	10	2	3		1	1	20		
9. Business Methods.	19		27	1	15	3	10	12	87	2/Lt. W.H. HAMBLYN.	
10. Mechanics 'E' Theory of Engines.	-	5	20		3		5	4	37		
11. Motor Mechanics.	11	43	43	2			20	2	121		Lt. JOHNSTON, R.
12. Electricity & Magnetism.		18	18		2		2	9	49		Lt. HEYLS, F.T. R.E.
13. Telephony & Telegraph.	1		4		1		2	5	13		
14. Chemistry & Physics.	1		9		4		1		15		L/C. PARSONS, Devons Pte. TUCKER, S.L.I. Capt. EDWARDS, R.H.
15. Building Construction.	3		5		1		7		16	2/Lt. LOUTIT, J.C.	
16. Machine Drawing.			12		4		4		20		
17. Agriculture & Gardening.	22		56	2		1	5	4	90		C.S.M. BICKLEY, J. Sgt. FOSS, Devons L/C. DUNNING, do 2nd Lt. DAVIDSON.
18. Drawing, Art & Design 'F'.	1		6		2	1	3		13		

Sheet No.2.

Unit.	16th Devons.	12th S.L.I.	14th R.H.	229th L.T.M.B.	229th F.Amb.	448th A.S.C.	439th R.E.	Bde. H.Q.	Total	Lecturers.	Instructors.
First Aid 'G'	3		3			1	1		8	Sgt.Youngs Lt.Arnott.	Devons R.H.
Veterinary Science.	66	3	18		1	1	4	4	97		
Book-keeping 'H'	2		1		1		1	2	7		
Poultry Farming.	6		5	2	1		5	1	20		
Shoemaking 'J'	1		6	1			1	1	10		
Tailoring.				1	1		1		3	Pte. PYM,	Devons
Haircutting.	1		2				2		5	Cpl.OLIVER, Pte.TREZISE,	Devons "
Cookery.	3		2						5	Cpl.MIKE, L.	Devons
Horse Shoeing.	13		7				1		21		
Simple Carpentry.	3		1		1		1		6		
Fitters.	2	5	2	1	1			1	12	Sgt.WALKER,	
Carpenters.	3	5	2	1	1		10	1	23	Pte.SOUTHERN Cpl.CHEERS,	Devons R.E.
Wheelers.	1		1						2		
Painters.			3				4		7		
Glaziers.											
Smiths.			1						1		
Coppersmiths.							1		1		
Bricklayers.	3								3		
Masons.	3		1				1	1	6		
Plumbers.			1		1		6	6	14	Cpl.HUGHS,	R.E.
Motor Mechanics.	5	18	10	1	5		7	1	47		
Motor Driving.	6		49	-	1	2	3	4	65		

Army Form C. 2118.

Jan 1919

WAR DIARY
or
INTELLIGENCE SUMMARY.

(Erase heading not required.)

Headquarters, 229th Infantry Brigade.

Instructions regarding War Diaries and Intelligence Summaries are contained in F. S. Regs., Part II. and the Staff Manual respectively. Title pages will be prepared in manuscript.

Copy.

Place	Date	Hour	Summary of Events and Information	Remarks and references to Appendices
Ref. Map Sheet 30. 1/40,000.	1919. January.			
GRAMMONT	7		Presentation of Medal Ribbons by G.O.C. 74th (Yeo) Division in Market Square.	
	22		Final of Divl. Cup - Association Football, 14th Royal Hdrs. versus 74th M.G. Battn. Result 14th R.H. 3; M.G.Bn. 0.	
	25		12th Som. L.I. enbussed for BRUSSELS, going into Billets at ANDERLECT.	
	26		12th Somerset L.I. forming part of 74th Divl. Composite Bde. marched past His Majesty the King of the BELGIANS.	
	28		12th Somerset L.I. returned from BRUSSELS.	
			Educational Scheme carried on throughout the month.	
			601 all ranks proceeded to U.K. for Demobilization during the month.	

4-2-19.

Kingsley
Captain,
Brigade Major,
229th Infantry Brigade.

Jan 1919

Army Form C. 2118.
Copy.

WAR DIARY
INTELLIGENCE SUMMARY.
(Erase heading not required.)

229 T.M.B JANUARY 1919

Place	Date	Hour	Summary of Events and Information	Remarks and references to Appendices
			REF MAP BELGIUM Sheet 30.1. 40,000	
GRAMMONT P.2.A.5.6.	Jan'y 1		BATTERY.	
	" 7		1.O.R. proceeded to U.K. for Demobilization	
	" 8		2.O.Rs	"	
	" 14		1.O.R	"	
	" 23		2.O.Rs	"	
	" 27		3.O.Rs	"	
	" 31		1.O.R	"	
			Educational Classes Group "A" & C. carried on during the month, but Group C. had to be suspended owing to Students being demobilized	

R.W. DeSerisee Lieut
O.C. 229th Inf. Bde
T.M Battery

WAR DIARY
or
INTELLIGENCE SUMMARY.

Headquarters, 229th Infantry Brigade.

(Erase heading not required.)

Army Form C. 2118.

February, 1919.

Instructions regarding War Diaries and Intelligence Summaries are contained in F.S. Regs., Part II. and the Staff Manual respectively. Title pages will be prepared in manuscript.

Place	Date	Hour	Summary of Events and Information	Remarks and references to Appendices
Ref. Map Sheet 30. 1/40,000.				
GRAMMONT.	1919. Feb.		Military, Recreational and Educational Training continued throughout month.	
			11 Officers, and 675 O.R. proceeded to U.K. for Demobilization during the month.	
	7-3-19.			

Kenyon Reamy

for Captain,
Brigade Major,
229th Infantry Brigade.

229 T.M.O.
Army Form C. 2118.

229th T.M. Battery

WAR DIARY

INTELLIGENCE SUMMARY.

(Erase heading not required.)

Place	Date	Hour	Summary of Events and Information	Remarks and references to Appendices
			FEBRUARY 1919.	
Ref. BELGIUM Sheet 30 1/40.000	Feb			
GRAMMONT.	1		2. O.R. demobilised whilst on 14 days ordinary leave in U.K.	and
V.A.&G.	7		3 O.R. demobilised whilst on 14 days ordinary leave in U.K.	and
	7		3. O.R. proceeded to U.K. for demobilisation.	and
	8		2. O.R. proceeded to U.K. for demobilisation.	and
	11		1. O.R. proceeded to U.K. for demobilisation.	and
	13		2. O.R. proceeded to U.K. for demobilisation.	(Occupation) and
	13		5. O.R. from 18th Bn. Somerset L.I. were returned to their unit for duty with the Armies of	and
	13		3. O.R. from 16th Bn. Devonshire Regt were returned to their unit for duty with the Armies of Occupation.	and
	15		2. O.R. proceeded to U.K. for demobilisation.	and
	15		Owing to the demobilisation of students Education classes in all subjects were closed.	and
	19		2nd Lieut. J.C. LOUTET. Struck off effective strength (Auth: Fifth Army N⁰ A 60/785.)	and
	20		2. O.R. proceeded to U.K. for demobilisation.	and
	21		2. O.R. proceeded to U.K. for demobilisation.	and

Army Form C. 2118.

WAR DIARY
or
INTELLIGENCE SUMMARY.
(Erase heading not required.)

229th L.I.M.B.

Instructions regarding War Diaries and Intelligence Summaries are contained in F. S. Regs., Part II. and the Staff Manual respectively. Title pages will be prepared in manuscript.

Place	Date	Hour	Summary of Events and Information	Remarks and references to Appendices
Ref BELGIUM Shet 30. 1/40,000:	Feb.		FEBRUARY 1919.	
GRAMMONT. V.2.a.55.	26.		2. O.R. despatched to U.K. for demobilisation.	

O.C. 229th L.M. Bttn

CONFIDENTIAL.

Headquarters,
　74th (Yeo) Division.

　　　　　Herewith War Diaries for the month of March.

　　　　　　　　　　　　　　[signature]
　　　　　　　　　　　　　　　　Captain,
　　　　　　　　　　　　　for Brigade Major,
　　　　　　　　　　　　229th Infantry Brigade.

4-4-19.

March, 1919.

Ref. Map Sheet 30. 1/40,000.

Army Form C. 2118.

WAR DIARY
or
INTELLIGENCE SUMMARY.
(Erase heading not required.)

HEADQUARTERS, 229th Infty. Bde.

Place	Date	Hour	Summary of Events and Information	Remarks and references to Appendices
GRAMMONT.	1919 March.		All training ceased during month owing to Demobilization.	
			Volunteers and Retainable Officers and O.R., under A.O. XIV, 16th (Yeo) Battn. Devonshire Regt. and 12th (Yeo) Battn. Somerset Light Infty. despatched to 2/4th Battn. Oxford and Bucks Light Infty. for Army of Occupation. Volunteers and Retainable Officers and O.R. under A.O. XIV from 14th Royal Hdrs. despatched to 6th and 8th Battn. Black Watch.	
			229th L.T.M.B. reduced to Cadre and affiliated to 16th Battn. Devonshire Regt.	
			15 Officers and 128 O.R. proceeded to U.K. for Demobilization during month.	
	11 Mar.		Brig. Genl. F.S. THACKERAY, D.S.O., M.C., proceeded on leave to U.K. from 11th to 28th March.	
	31		Brig. Genl. F.S. THACKERAY, D.S.O., M.C., Highland L.I., ordered to the Rhine, to Command 6th Battn. Kings Own Scottish Borders.	
			Captain A.J.M. TUCK, M.C., Seaforth Highlanders, Brigade Major, - cross-posted Brigade Major, 231 Infantry Brigade, to date from 22-3-19.	

4-4-19.

[signature]
Captain,
for Brigade Major,
229th Infantry Brigade.

Headquarters.
74th. (Yeo) Division.

> HEADQUARTERS
> 229TH INFANTRY BDE
> Date 5-5-19
> Ref. No. 47

Herewith War Diaries for the month of April.

P Kenyon Slaney

Captain,
for Lt. Col. Commdg.
229th. INfantry Brigade.

5/5/19.

Army Form C. 2118

WAR DIARY
or
INTELLIGENCE SUMMARY
(Erase heading not required.)

Instructions regarding War Diaries and Intelligence Summaries are contained in F. S. Regs., Part II. and the Staff Manual respectively. Title Pages will be prepared in manuscript.

Place	Date	Hour	Summary of Events and Information	Remarks and references to Appendices
Grammont. Belgium.	1919. April.		Headquarters. 229th. Infantry Brigade.	
			Brigade reduced to Cadre "A" Establishment.	
			All animals evacuated during month.	

WAR DIARY
INTELLIGENCE SUMMARY.
(Erase heading not required.)

Army Form C. 2118.

WO 229 Inf Bde /14

Place	Date	Hour	Summary of Events and Information	Remarks and references to Appendices
GRAMMONT (BELGIUM)	1919 MAY		229" Infantry Brigade Hqrs.	
	4.		Instructions received that cadre of Inf. Bde would be reduced to 3 Officers and 36 O.R. Personnel available for disposal on above reduction despatched for demobilization	
	9.		1st Class D.D. OGILVIE 14' Bn Royal Highlanders returned from Cairo in U.K. and resumed command of Bde. camp	
	15.			
	29.		Instructions received that then issued to a further reduction of cadre by 75% of original establishment as shown in Appendix 2. Part 3 Army Demobilization Instructions France. Cadre of each Inf. Bde. was now composed of 1 Officer and 12 O.R. – Cadre of Brig de Hqrs. 1 Officer and 3 O.R.	

O. Hua Capt
Staff Capt
229 Inf Bde.

HEADQUARTERS
229th INFANTRY BDE.
Date 25/6/19
Ref No. 47

Hqrs
74th (Yeo) Div

Herewith War Diary of these Hqrs and for 13 Bn. Somerset L.I. for month of June.

A Hieaut Capt
Staff Capt
229 Inf Bde

25/6/19

WAR DIARY
or
INTELLIGENCE SUMMARY
(Erase heading not required.)

Army Form C. 2118.

WO 229 Infantry Brigade 1/9/15

Place	Date	Hour	Summary of Events and Information	Remarks and references to Appendices
GRAMMONT (BELGIUM)	1919 JUNE		229th Infantry Brigade.	
	4.		Instruction received that Cadres of the three Bns would proceed home with equipment, leaving behind an equipment guard of 2 officers and 12 O.R. who would travel with the equipment to ENGLAND.	
	16.		Cadre of 16 Bn. Worc. Regt and 13 Bn. Somerset L.I. eff GRAMMONT for CONCENT ONE, LILLE en route for demobilization.	
	19.		Cadre of 1st Bn. Royal Highlanders eff GRAMMONT for CONCENT ONE, LILLE en route for demobilization.	
	21.		All equipment of 229 Bde Hqrs handed in to I.C.S.S. ATH.	
	23.		Entrainment of equipment guards of the three Bns commenced at 10.00 hrs. Train eff GRAMMONT for ANTWERP at 12.30. completed at 17.00.	

O.H. Beard Capt
Staff Capt
229 Inf Bde.

www.ingramcontent.com/pod-product-compliance
Lightning Source LLC
Chambersburg PA
CBHW081354160426
43192CB00013B/2406